Troping
the Body

Troping the Body

Gender,

Etiquette, and

Performance

Gwendolyn Audrey Foster

Southern Illinois University Press
Carbondale and Edwardsville

Library of Congress Cataloging-in-Publication Data
Foster, Gwendolyn Audrey.
  Troping the body : gender, etiquette, and performance / Gwendolyn
Audrey Foster.
    p.   cm.
  Includes bibliographical references and index.
  1. Etiquette. 2. Man-woman relationships. I. Title.
BJ1853.F62 2000
395'.01—dc21
ISBN 0-8093-2286-2 (alk. paper)   99-38549
ISBN 0-8093-2287-0 (pbk. : alk. paper)   CIP

The paper used in this publication meets the minimum requirements of
American National Standard for Information Sciences—Permanence of
Paper for Printed Library Materials, ANSI Z39.48-1992. ♾

Contents

Preface

This book grew out of my fascination with etiquette books and conduct literature. In a graduate seminar led by Susan Rosowski, I expressed my interest in writing a paper examining the role of women as etiquette writers. I proposed such a project to my professor and peers, explaining my fascination with a whole range of popular literature on etiquette, manners, dress, behavior, and charm. I had difficulty defining the scope of my study because, to me, there was no clear boundary between high literature and the literature of popular culture. I have always been interested in women writers, race, gender, and power, but I felt I had stumbled on an area that was seemingly ignored; specifically, I was interested in the possibility of locating power and agency in the voices of popular etiquette writers, such as Emily Post and, more recently, Martha Stewart. My classmates were eager to foster discussion on the politics of this power, and they were extremely helpful in bringing to my attention the value of such a project. I brought a number of examples of etiquette and conduct texts to class and discussed my attraction and repulsion to these texts, many of which were blatantly racist, sexist, classist, homophobic, and patently offensive in every way from a cultural perspective. I described my feelings about these books to the class, most of whom clearly chose to write about authors whom they loved. I said I both loved and hated these books, and I found them macabre, humorous in the fashion most associated with camp. Nevertheless, I wanted to get beyond the humor I found in these books to the core of power involved in essentially telling people how to behave, from instructions on how to set a table to how to make conversation at a dinner party.

At this point, there were two studies that had a great deal of influence on me in terms of setting my scope and defining my methodology. *Women and Power in the Middle Ages* was influential in my thinking because the authors encouraged and rehearsed a new way of interpreting the various local heterogemonies of power held by women that had not yet been recognized as areas of power because power has been defined largely by patriarchal hegemonic thinking. I talked about the issue of power in the role of social arbiter with my peers and colleagues and found that many seemed uncomfortable with the idea that some women had held powerful roles as etiquette writers. The discomfort arises when we are confronted with the racism, classism, sexism, homophobia, and various other offensive social constructions that are often institutionalized and perpetuated in popular etiquette and conduct literature. I got the distinct message that, as a feminist, it would indeed be problematic to write about women writers who wielded influence and power in ways that have not always been helpful to women. Around this time, a study of women in the Ku Klux Klan was published. *Women of the Klan*, by Kathleen M. Blee, was helpful in the task of unraveling the complexities of our Foucaultian notions of power and finding that some women have indeed been active throughout history as agents of power in institutions that are revolting and irredeemable. I wrote the study despite and perhaps because of my unusual reaction to etiquette and conduct texts. I submitted the article for publication and was not surprised to find that, for the editor, the thorniest issue I brought up was women's power as social arbiters. I was asked to tone down my remarks about the role of some women as exemplifications of a nexus of power that some women have exerted in a whole range of popular advice books, from the medieval texts of Christine de Pizan, to the current classist texts of Martha Stewart.

I was disturbed to find that most studies of women writers confined themselves to celebratory studies of politically astute women writers who went against the grain of the hegemonic power structures of various patriarchal cultural institutions. However, I think this has changed as a result of rethinking power and rethinking the literature of power, specifically with the numerous feminist reinterpretations of Foucault, from the fields of cultural studies, queer studies, postcolonial studies, performance studies, gender studies, various schools of film studies, popular culture studies, and literary studies.

I immersed myself in the study of power and came away convinced that power is tied not only to institutions and their purveyors but also to the corporeal body, specifically performativity. I began to see that social correction and etiquette writing went beyond the boundaries of the popular texts of Emily Post. I began to see that male and female writers have been offering advice and performing the body in the poetry of Emily Brontë, for example, or the romantic poets. I had been collecting all sorts of etiquette books, and I began to see etiquette as it is performed in literature and film. All around me, I found instructional texts or the instructional voices in the texts I read and watched, from Karen Finley's performance art to Jesse Helms's routine corrective "advice" to the nation as legislator. I found it exciting to begin to view the etiquette playing field as a place of jockeying for power in terms of gender, race, and class. Men and women have been wrestling for the role of social arbiter from, no doubt, even before the Middle Ages.

Nevertheless, I found that the main players in the Middle Ages and the Renaissance were well known, at least within academic studies. Norbert Elias, in *The History of Manners*, charts the European white tradition of courtliness, etiquette, and manners in writers such as Erasmus, and I was already quite aware of the powerful role of men such as Machiavelli. I located a useful anthology edited by Nancy Armstrong and Leonard Tennenhouse on the ideology of conduct books. This book was influential in my thinking about the role of etiquette and conduct writers, especially with regard to the politics of gender and questions of power as it is performed in corrective literature.

Anyone interested in etiquette and conduct is bound to find herself or himself interested in gesture and the literature of gesture, especially the early instructional manuals on gesture. These handbooks specifically articulate how one should hold one's body, as a speaker, for example, how one should gesture during a speech, and so on. Clearly, the study of gesture is closely related to the study of performance and performativity. In this area, I found several studies particularly useful and incisive.

An early model in performance studies, Marco de Marinis's *The Semiotics of Performance* was particularly helpful for me in that I began to see that the power dynamics performed in various texts and contexts are themselves made complex by more ontological concerns. In other words, etiquette texts both provoke the real and describe the real; they duplicate power structures as much as they participate in them, or as de Marinis writes, "[P]erformance always provokes effects of the real as well as theatrical effects . . . in the sense of its real production of meanings, kinds of awareness, events, and lived experience" (157).

A groundbreaking anthology that made me rethink the boundaries and methodologies of this book was *Performing Feminisms: Feminist Critical Theory and Theatre*, which included essays written by Judith Butler and Sue-Ellen Case. Butler, Case, Phelan, Sedgwick, and other queer performative theorists have transformed feminist cultural studies and made possible new ways of analyzing power relationships and dynamics beyond essentialist politics in ways I wish had been available to me when I first embarked on this study.

The postcolonial theorists who have had a remarkable influence over my thoughts include bell hooks, Homi Bhabha, Fatimah Tobing Rony, and many others, who helped me to understand that African American women writers and filmmakers have seized power as social arbiters, not necessarily in the same manner as Emily Post, Amy Vanderbilt, or Martha Stewart, but more in the manners of Phillis Wheatley, Harriet Wilson,

Bessie Smith, Alice Walker, Frances E. W. Harper, Toni Morrison, and Oprah Winfrey.

The aim and scope of this book has shifted considerably since I first conceived of it. I therefore examine not only etiquette and conduct books, but also a host of texts that may be considered as such. I have not limited myself in terms of race or gender. The texts I have chosen were published in different historical periods, from the Middle Ages up to the present. In *Troping the Body,* I redefine the boundaries of conduct literature through a theoretical examination of the gendered body as it is positioned in conduct books, etiquette texts, poetry, fiction, and film. I draw upon Bakhtin, Gates, Foucault, and the new school of performative feminism to develop an interdisciplinary approach to conduct literature and literature as conduct.

Acknowledgments

I wish to thank the UNL Research Council for their fiscal support of this project in the form of a 1998 summer stipend. I am indebted to many of my colleagues here at the University of Nebraska Department of English. I wish to thank both Stephen Hilliard, chair of the Department of English during my first years at the university, and Linda Ray Pratt, current chair of the Department of English, for their unstinting support of my research projects.

I wish to extend special thanks to Susan Rosowski, who has seen this book evolve and develop over a number of years. I thank her for her support and enthusiasm. I also must thank Steve Buhler for his remarks on the chapter on Isabella Whitney. Tom Bestul was most helpful and instructive in my research into medieval conduct literature, especially that of Christine de Pizan. Sharon Harris read and commented on the chapter on Hannah Webster Foster. I thank Sharon for making me aware of the multitude of women writers who asserted themselves as moral instructors in the rapidly developing "civilization" of early America. Steve Behrendt helped me mine my way through the Victorian period, which was rife with instructional literature. Maureen Honey read and commented on the chapter on Virginia Woolf and Edith Wharton. Maureen was especially receptive and perceptive on the notion of performativity.

I am also deeply grateful to many libraries, research centers, archives, and museums and their staff, including the Museum of Modern Art Film Department, Gaumont Films in Paris, the New York Public Library, and the Black Film Center Archive at Indiana University. I thank the members of UNL interlibrary loan.

I wish to thank the editors of *Text and Performance Quarterly* for permission to reprint "Troping the Body: Etiquette Texts and Performance," which was previously published in *TPQ* 13.1 (January 1993): 79–96; used by permission of the National Communication Association. Thanks to the *Journal of the American Studies Association of Texas* for permission to reprint "The Dialogic Margins of Conduct Fiction: Hannah

Webster Foster's *The Boarding School*," originally published in *JASAT* 25 (October 1994): 59–72.

My sincere thanks to Dana Miller for her help in typing this manuscript in its many successive drafts and forms. I also wish to thank her for her professional support and to recognize her as a role model as an activist. I want to thank Dana for helping me keep my sense of humor through the long and arduous task of creating this manuscript.

I wish to thank my husband, Wheeler Winston Dixon, for his many acts of kindness and support, his loving help in everything from manuscript preparation to fostering nascent ideas (quite often in the middle of the night). It is impossible to list all the ways in which creative partners support one another's work. Suffice it to say that Wheeler and I probably spend equal amounts of time rereading, commenting on, and talking about one another's projects as we do enacting them. No one could find a more supportive partner, much less a more enthusiastic soul mate.

This book is dedicated to the late Leslie Kaliades.

Troping
the Body

1
Etiquette Texts and Performance

In 1792, Mary Wollstonecraft began chapter 8 ("Morality Undermined by Sexual Notions of the Importance of a Good Reputation") of her book *A Vindication of the Rights of Woman* with the following remarks: "It has long since occurred to me that advice respecting behavior, and all the various modes of preserving a good reputation, which have been so strenuously inculcated on the female world, were specious poisons" (144). According to Wollstonecraft, etiquette leads both men and women to "acquire, from a supposed necessity, an equally artificial mode of behavior" (144). Yet, she continues, "the two sexes mutually corrupt and improve each other. . . . Chastity, modesty, public spirit, and all the noble train of virtues, on which social virtue and happiness are built, should be understood and cultivated by all mankind, or they will be cultivated to little effect" (153).

Thus, Wollstonecraft views the socializing influence of the code of etiquette with obvious distrust and calls instead for a more "natural" order. Wollstonecraft inadvertently argues for regulation of the gendered self under an ideological system that was, in the nineteenth century, preoccupied with transforming the performing self, and the grotesque desires of the body, into an aestheticized version of the "natural" self, a gilded body at times indistinguishable from a decorated home. Ironically, etiquette and conduct manuals textually authenticate a quest that has been located by cultural critic Carol Houlihan Flynn "for a lost unity of body and soul, sense and reason that could only exist in an Edenic imagination" (73). These texts exhibit striking similarity, then, with interior decorating texts of the Victorian period, which have been identified as strategic sites of Victorian "self performance through authentication" (Twigg 3) that "reproduced the fragmented and hollow nature of the Victorian self," as Reginald Twigg accurately observes, "precisely because it was a mask" (17).

The fragmentation of the performing body in the utopic, idealized home reveals an ideological concern with maintenance of gender, race, and class order, especially as it is located in the problematic desires of the body. The containment of desire in the bodies of the members of the rising working class by the dominant ruling class is predicated upon strict adherence to gendered and class-stratified order and, as Nancy Armstrong and Leonard Tennenhouse have argued, etiquette and conduct literature writers are intensely hegemonic, just as they pose themselves as politically neutral, and they reflect a systematic aestheticization of the culturally approved forms of desire (1–2).

While the illustrative matter in etiquette books quite often represents the domestic site itself (place settings, living room arrangements), the body of the reader receives discipline from the author, who continually regulates the desired performance in a manner that obsequiously urges reader identification through textual strategies designed to submit her to a system in which she is consistently urged to deny the "natural" self. One particularly important reason for a critical examination of the popular etiquette book is that the performance of etiquette allows for the signification of gendered roles that are "engendered before being fixed in the world" or, from a theoretical standpoint, exist in a metalinguistic sphere much like the "language of gestures" described by Julia Kristeva (*Language* 303, 304).

Bakhtin would describe the phenomena as a denial of the "grotesque" body in favor of an embrace of the "classical" or rational, chaste, socialized one. Throughout etiquette books of the last century, the performing self, or reader, is expected to transcend the experience of the body in its Rousseauian state. The writers of these texts rarely updated this Victorian schema, even with changing social expectations. If contemporary critical theory examines these charged zones of "power and space" in societal discourse, it is the etiquette text that first created them. And it is important to note that, in most cases, these texts were written by women.

Through a cultural analysis of the symbols of the etiquette book, we may begin to unravel the ideological campaign of the quest for (utopic) tasteful behavior. I analyze sites in the etiquette text in which the performing body is construed as a figure in danger of succumbing to its supposedly grotesque nature, in cases of social mutability, interracial behavior, dining, and sexuality. Finally, I address female authorship of etiquette texts as an exhibition of the writing of the female body as a locus of desire for control over performance of the body of the self and others. Initially, however, I briefly place the issue of authority and the dialogic and metonymical textual strategies of etiquette writers in historical perspective.

For the Victorian female etiquette authority, the body of the reader is a ready and willing receiver of discipline. Having positioned herself as an authority on behavior, the voice of the etiquette writer assumes a dominant and authoritarian stance through the use of a number of distinctive linguistic devices. The etiquette writer usually speaks to the reader in sweeping declarative statements. For example, "[N]o guest may leave after a formal dinner in a private home in less than two and a half to three hours" (Vanderbilt 276). Alternatively, she poses a rhetorical question and then provides the answer clearly, if glibly, as if anyone of "class" should already know the only possible "correct" answer. "Wrong" and "right" are easy to discern in the voice of the etiquette writer, who often assumes an intimate relationship with the reader that allows for "nagging," as in "[H]ave you written that note?" (Sprackling 94). Adopting an omniscient tone, the etiquette writer even uses Biblical references, such as these "Business Commandments. . . . Be prompt. Do not resent criticism. Even if you think it unfair, be grateful for it. Capitalize on it" (Sprackling 250).

The voice of the etiquette writer can console, validate, or chasten the reader, assuming a personal relationship not unlike that of an older, and presumably wiser, family member. Quite often, these books contain self-quizzes, or dialogical displays of the intertextuality of the authority of the writer, asking, for example, "[W]hat would you do . . . if you spilled jam on the table cloth at a dinner party?" (Stratton and Schleman 121). This "self-quiz" structure is a common device found also in general circulation magazines and behavioral guidebooks. A charm school handbook demands, for example "[D]o you have at least two dresses with exceptionally flattering necklines?" (Taylor, n.p.). The use of these stratagems fosters the teacher/student model of instruction in etiquette texts, with the submissive reader, eager for instruction, listening raptly to the metonymic answers of authority. In a critical reading, of course, the spell of this relationship is broken, since the critic only poses as the reader and refuses to succumb to the spell of the text.

One reason for the success of Emily Post is her persistent and emotionally astute use of narratives involving a cast of intertextual performers whose highly descriptive names included "Mrs. Cravin Praise," "Mrs. Newly Rich," "Mrs. Gilding," "Mrs. Kindhart," "Mr. and Mrs. Oneroom," and, of course, the ideal personage, "Mrs. Worldly." As one example of a highly charged narrative, Post's cautionary tale, "How a Dinner Can Be Bungled," is effectively plotted and dramatically punctuated with humor and pathos.

"How a Dinner Can Be Bungled" is preceded by a story of the perfect dinner at the Worldlys'. "You . . . a young socially inexperienced bride" (in Post's words) decide to throw a formal dinner party. Your cook and hired help bungle everything. You barely have enough silver to set a proper table, and just as the guests arrive, you light the fireplace. Post picks up the narrative: "As 'Mr. Clubwin Doe' enters, the room looks charming, then suddenly the fire smokes, and as the smoke gets thicker your other guests arrive. Everyone begins to cough and blink." The disastrous dinner continues as the maid, "Sigrid" (presumably a nonwhite servant), shouts obnoxiously, "Dinner's all ready!" Predictably, the food is terrible, the conversation is cutting, and "you" are socially ruined (*Post's Etiquette* 180–83).

The point of view of the narrative is especially effective because Post postures the body of the reader at the center of the story. As a form of literature, the etiquette text stands outside of any literary canon, yet its ideological underpinning shares many of the concerns of other forms of popular culture in the American middle class, such as movies, magazines, pulp fiction, and advertisements, "familial" texts (Hodge and Kress 221) that seek to perpetuate the desired order of the family.

Etiquette writers in industrialized America posed as authorities on taste, or more accurately aestheticized the performing body, which was in reality often placed in uncomfortable situations of novelty, due to social mobility. Through the legislation of conformity in performance, etiquette writers promised ease in movement between social spheres. The derivation of the word *etiquette,* from the Old French *estiquette* meaning "ticket" (OAD 413), evolved from courtly society, when it was necessary to have a ticket to enter court. By 1948, Millicent Fenwick, author of *Vogue's Book of Etiquette: A Complete Guide to Traditional Forms of Modern Usage,* said etiquette was no longer a set of rules for "the inner circle"; rather, it had supposedly evolved into a set of social standards to be observed by all. Fenwick noted, "In the last twenty years, particularly in America, etiquette has become less arbitrary and more democratic. . . . There is no longer any question of admission 'by ticket only.' . . . Good behavior is everybody's business, and good taste can be everyone's goal" (3).

Historically, of course, the outward control of the body and the emphasis on appearances can be traced to the etiquette in court society, which emphasized the importance of the "advantages of noble birth" (Aresty 64). The term *courtesy* tellingly reflects much about the history of "good" behavior and its ties to early "court" society. Courtesy as defined by the *American College Dictionary,* is not only "1) excellence of manners or behavior; politeness. 2) a courteous act or expression. 3) Favor; indulgence; consent: a title by courtesy rather than by right"; it is also seen as an act of social deference, "4) a curtsy" (278).

Curtsy, in turn, is defined by the *Oxford American Dictionary* as "a bow by women in recognition or respect, consisting of bending the knees and lowering the body" (298), a sex-role defined code of behavior. The root of the word *court,* from the Latin word *cohors* for "enclosure" (278) neatly demonstrates the exclusionary socio-economic roots of courtly behavior. This is important to note, for American etiquette writers would seek to change this elitism in their attempts to "democratize" etiquette.

In the opening remarks of most etiquette books, one finds definitions of etiquette as, for example from a 1942 volume, "consideration of your fellow human beings," (McCrady and Wheeler v). Usually, there follows a sort of promise of social "leveling-up" through etiquette, as in this example from 1942: "The behavior of the $12 a week stenographer can be just as becoming as that of the $50,000 a year lady" (McCrady and Wheeler v). As further proof of this democratic instinct, in the introduction to Emily Post's first book, Richard Duffy, Post's editor at Funk and Wagnalls, uses careful wording to suggest the possibility of equality through etiquette. He says that "etiquette is no flummery of poseurs 'aping the manners of their betters,' nor a code of snobs . . . but a system of rules of conduct based on respect of self coupled with respect of others" (xvii). Yet this seeming "leveling" of the classes is, in many respects, illusory. Folklorist Gerald Carson concluded that when etiquette "manual writers offered such entreé [into society] they promised something they could not deliver . . . [that] aristocratic privilege could be had at a price; but not at the price of an etiquette book" (183–84).

Nevertheless, Emily Post rebuts this criticism in answering her question "What Is Best Society?," as "not a fellowship of the wealthy but . . . an association of gentle-folk" (*Post's Etiquette* 3), in which manners, preferably of the deferential sort, constitute the price of admission. Annegret S. Ogden notes that the "Ladies Magazines" of the nineteenth century "translate[d] the undemocratic, feudal notions of nobility and *noblesse oblige* for the average American consumer" (50). Society clung to the values of Victorian culture that espoused "weakness as strength" as a platitude toward women and continued the subtext that "every American home had the potential to be made into a castle by a clever decorator" (Ogden 50). Gender expectations were increasingly polarized, just as class expectations were seemingly harmonized. Ogden concludes that "to this very day, the ladies' magazines hold their readers by appealing to the hidden Victorian in them all—the one who craves . . . the doll house existence of the perfect lady and gentleman" (51).

Just as the "castle" has enormous potential for masquery by the "clever decorator," so the table in the "doll house" can be set to the strict requirements of the iconographic place settings from the pages of the etiquette book. In this respect, at least, one may aspire to, and achieve, perfection. In our daily manners, we restrict ourselves with the same sort of psychic Victorian "corseting," partitioning off desire from our social existence. These manifestations of Victorian fetishism in etiquette function as a metaphoric "chastity belt," rigidly defining the boundaries of social respectability and disciplining the performing self within these boundaries.

Thomas Kochman posits that "upon closer examination, one might see that mainstream American protocols might not, in fact, be all that impartial. Rather, as with most established systems, such protocols can be seen as serving the interests of those who have installed them" (201). Thus, Kochman sees the power of etiquette as "administrative" in his examination of the basis for codes of social governance. He takes the popular definition of etiquette, "showing consideration for the feelings of others" (205), and through an analysis of the term *others*, he finds that "within mainstream etiquette, there is a sociocultured bias, or predisposition, in favor of low-keyed assertive public behavior" (207). Kochman, an African American, sees etiquette as a form of social propaganda. "Mainstream American etiquette accomplishes socially what mainstream American society wishes to accomplish politically . . . [so that] established authority can exercise its power with a minimum of resistance and/or risk" (208). In this analysis, Kochman correctly identifies one of the most surreptitious aspects of the etiquette book. In its insidious display of behavioral authority, the voice of the etiquette writer speaks in defense of the continued enfranchisement of the existing social order, at the expense of the marginalized minorities who do not benefit, directly or indirectly, from the perpetuation of the status quo.

That manners, or "low-keyed assertive public behavior," are necessary to provide order in a world of suppressed savagery seems a common source of pride for the etiquette writer. After all, it is in the best interest of the etiquette writer to preserve the primacy of the status quo. Judith Martin, syndicated as the newspaper columnist "Miss Manners," attacked the lack of manners in modern society in her speech of 1984 at Harvard University, insisting that "the lack of standardization of manners results in an anger-ridden, chaotic society" (35). She berates natural behavior as "the Jean Jacques Rousseau school of etiquette" and notes that "many forms of etiquette are employed precisely to disguise those antipathies that arise from irreconcilable differences, in order to prevent mayhem" (35).

Although Martin displays a parodic voice in her writing, at base she is absolutely serious; without the socializing voice of the etiquette writer, she feels, a complete overthrow of the existing social order would result. Promoters of etiquette as a civilizing good force undoubtedly would disagree with sociologist Joanne Finkelstein, who sees manners in an unflattering light, labeling them "instruments of concealed interests" (135), particularly as they are used in dining out. According to Finkelstein, the deference we show waiters, and vice versa, "may be seen as a mechanism which divorces the interactants from a close examination of their conduct." Further, "the display of deference, in this instance, can divert us from seeing how status and power deferentials are negotiated between strangers and why personal pleasure is attached to this exchange" (141).

Bakhtin, writing as V. N. Volosinov, noted this difference between the interior and exterior spheres of performance when he wrote that "each person's inner world and thought has its stabilized social audience that comprises the environment in which reasons, motives, values and so on are fashioned . . . specific class and specific era are limits that the ideal of addressee cannot go beyond" (*Marxism* 86). The etiquette writer is engaged in describing the boundaries of potential trespass, in mapping the territory between the "inner world" and the "stabilized social audience" that world must serve.

In *The Care of the Self*, Michel Foucault examines some of the ways in which the female body is constrained by the marriage contract and by the societal rules that, oddly enough, have been inculcated and in many cases originated by feminine role models. Specifically, Foucault sees marriage as "a stronger force for binding conjugal partners and hence a more effective one for isolating the couple in a field of social relations" (*Care* 77). This "isolation" of the couple from the society that surrounds it, which also ensures the isolation of each person within the "union" from each other (each to her or his own domain) is an essential part of the troping of the female body as a locus of desire and commodification.

Women reading etiquette texts were encouraged not only to observe gender defined behaviors designed to supposedly protect themselves but also to cultivate an affected air of solicitude (Kasson 147). In Post's 1922 etiquette manual, *Emily Post's Etiquette: In Society, in Business, in Politics and at Home*, Post includes an essay entitled "The Bow of a Woman of Charm." Post adopts a friendly conversational tone, encouraging women to "acquire a charming bow. It is such a short and fleeting duty. Not a bit of trouble really; just to incline your head and spontaneously smile as though you thought 'why, there is Mrs. Smith! How glad I am to see her!'" (26). Post reverts to her authoritarian stance when admonishing women to avoid attracting attention to themselves in public. "Do not expose your private affairs, feelings or innermost thoughts," wrote Post. "You are knocking down the walls of your house when you do" (29). Outward artifice and mannerly caution are presented as skills of social survival in a world in which the parameters of the woman and the house are for Post one and the same.

Curiously, Post is fond of blurring the distinctions between her definitions of women and houses. In several incidences, Post refers to women as houses or vice versa. Formal written invitations, carried over from the nineteenth century, supported the boundaries between the separate spheres. Post and other etiquette writers provided extensive examples of rules for invitations, the likes of which are seen only for wedding invitations in the 1990s. The formal calling system preserved the sanctity of the house, which was of central importance to the idealized vision of an American family, second only to the chastity of the American woman. When "Mrs. Gilding" or "Mrs. Worldly" requested "the honour" of one's presence or "the pleasure" of one's company, she, in effect, trusted you with her most intimate material and spiritual investment, her private sphere, over which she had labored and over which she charmingly and ceremoniously presided.

In the same text, Post is masterful in pleasing and catering to her audience of women of varying economic means in her chapters "The Well-Appointed House," "Formal Dinners," "Limited Equipment," and "Teas and Other Afternoon Parties." A maid is a prerequisite, however, for the "gem of a house." Its "bell . . . [should be] answered promptly by a trim maid with a low voice and quiet, courteous manners." But it is "Mrs. Worldly" whom middle-class women collectively inspire to emulate in Post's utopia. She "pays seemingly no attention, but nothing escapes her. She can walk through a room without appearing to look left or right, yet if the slightest detail is amiss, her house telephone is rung at once" (130, 131).

"Taste in selection of people" is "the first essential" toward worldliness, according to Post. Women must choose their dinner companions as carefully as men choose their employees. In this section, Post uses the voice of a parent, carefully explaining "Professor Bugge might bore you to tears, but Mrs. Entemoid would probably delight in him; just as Mr. Stocks and Bonds and Mrs. Rich would probably have interests in common" (186). The nouveau riche character "Mrs. New-To-Best-Society" is provided with extensive instructions to manage in her dealings with the "well-to-do characters . . . Mrs. Worldly" and "Mrs. Oldname." Having arrived in society, "Mrs. New-To-Best-Society" can enjoy the privileges accorded "Mrs. Worldly," a snob who invites such characters as "Oldworlds" but snubs the "Newell Riches." "Mrs. Worldly" is presented as trapped to some extent by her social standing; she can "afford" to invite only a few of her "real friends" who do not offend those for whom she wishes to perform.

Throughout *Emily Post's Etiquette: In Society, in Business, in Politics and at Home*, the practice and cultivation of outward affectation in performance is continually stressed. In "How to Walk Across a Ballroom" for example, Post deplores the behavior of the quintessential flapper, an "athletic young woman of to-day," who "strides across the ballroom floor as if she were on a golf course." Other women, Post complains, amble along, "shoulders stooped, arms swinging, hips and head in advance of chest." Post's description of the perfection of the gait of "Mrs. Oldname" suggests constraint, discomfort, and a constant pre-occupation with outward appearance: "Her body is perfectly balanced[,] . . . she holds herself straight[,] . . . she takes steps of medium length, and . . . [she] walks from the hip, not the knee. On no account does she swing her arms." Post clearly misses the Victorian past, when the "Toplofty's . . . made all their [female] grandchildren walk daily across a polished floor with sand-bags on their heads" (261–62). Post implies that the performance of grace not only makes a pleasing appearance but also protects a woman from physical harm.

Artificial performance is "What makes a young girl a ballroom success," Post explains. "Learned self-unconsciousness" is the best advice to "make herself believe that a good time exists in her own mind. If she can become possessed with the idea that she is having a good time and look as though she were, the psychological effect is astonishing" (268). This constant preoccupation with facial expressions, combined with a feigned state of mental balance, is reminiscent of the Victorian elocution guides, which provide extensive illustrations of proper physical gestures to be used in oral performance. Though young women are implored to master the gestures of a controlled actress, "a smile should be spontaneous . . . [because] nothing has less allure than a mechanical grimace" (284). A clear parallel exists between this feigned naturalness and "search for authenticity" described by Twigg (3) in Victorian decorative tastes and the museum facade of the rising middle class. This is the paradox: one must seem "natural" in society, lacking obvious performative gestures, yet one must simultaneously be continually conscious of rules and standards that oppressively mandate everyday social commerce. Thus, one is always on display, always striving for the real in the world of the artificial.

In a section of *Emily Post's Etiquette: In Society, in Business, in Politics and at Home* titled "Mrs. Grundy," Post conjures up a character who originated in the British play *Speed the Plough* and later became a popularly cited figure in nineteenth-century British etiquette books. Warning her female audience against this "disagreeable old woman," Post uses fairy tale imagery and language, anchoring her allegory in a Gothic setting. Mrs. Grundy is seen in a "brownstone house with a cupola used as a conning tower and equipped with periscope and telescope and wireless[,] . . . her house situated on a bleak hill so that nothing impedes her view and that of her two pets, a magpie and a jackal. The business in life of all three of them," warns Post, "is to track down and destroy the good name of every woman who comes within range, especially if she is young and pretty and unchaperoned." Against this evil spinster is set the example of the pretty young woman living alone," who, Post cautions, "must literally follow Cinderella's habits" (292). Thus, "Mrs. Grundy" becomes a regendered "Big Bad Wolf," threatening each innocent victim with slanderous innuendo rather than sexual and/or physical harm.

Post surreptitiously weaves in the sexual prejudices of earlier centuries as she admonishes "young and pretty and divorced women" to "literally live the life of a Puritan spinster of Salem" (294). Acknowledging the fear women are taught to have of losing their dignity, or worse, their chastity, Post paradoxically admits the near impossibility of maintaining such high standards of behavior. For there is no safe harbor for the single woman; she is judged not only by men but also by other women. Mrs. Grundy's "magpie never leaves her window sill [,] and the jackal sits on the doormat, and the news of her [the single or divorced woman] every coming in, of every one whom she receives, when they come, how long they stay and at what hour they go, is spread broadcast." In short, Post states, "no unprotected woman can do the least thing that is unconventional, without having Mrs. Grundy shouting to everyone the worst possible things about her" (294).

Post's description of a social order among women and men maintained through constant self-supervision and presided over by self-appointed members of Mrs. Grundy's army of etiquette police is much like one model of the modern prison, in which inmates are part of, and subject to, the enforcing gaze of an all-inclusive panoptic perspective. In the "panopticon" prison system, as Foucault notes in *Discipline and Punish,* dominance is attained through the medium of constant, unwavering supervision, which finds its ultimate expression in self-surveillance. The inmate thus enters "a state of conscious and permanent visibility that assures the automatic functioning of power" (*Discipline* 201). The individual is simultaneously trained to perform specific roles under this unrelenting external/internal supervision, with the result that a great deal of the power of such a system comes from within each individual prisoner.

Artificial performance, self-surveillance, and denial of the Bakhtinian grotesque (or sexual) body is of key importance as a female and/or male trope in Emily Post's texts. In *The Use of Pleasure,* Foucault identifies marriage as primarily an "economic" state rather than a social one, and maps out the varying exchanges of power and dominion proscribed by the traditional marital unit, in which the man attains social power over his wife, and within society as a whole, through means of sexual exclusivity and commodification of the "troped" female corpus (Foucault, *Use* 151). For Foucault, Bakhtin, and Post (an unlikely threesome), sexual role playing is primarily an exchange of power and status. Self-surveillance and denial of the "grotesque" body are thus key factors in maintaining the all-important social "stability" of the marital relationship within the society that supports and celebrates it.

In 1932, Alice Duer Miller concluded in an article in the *Saturday Evening Post* that manners, "like the bringing up of our children, have become the concern of the women of the household[, yet] . . . American women have not made a very good job of American society. . . . Let the executive genius of the American man have a chance. Conversation, I believe, would be more interesting and [men] would cease to be sulky aliens at their own parties and would become happier and, therefore, better mannered" (43). Miller's labeling of twentieth-century American men as "sulky aliens" in social intercourse implies a tension inherent between the performing bodies of the genders and the spheres they inherited from the nineteenth century, when "gender was the crucial distinction within any individual household as men went out to work and women stayed home" (Strasser 182). With women relegated to the unwanted role of social arbiter, men become the "other" or "outsider," looking in at the "matriarchal" family unit. Mainstream etiquette books, other than those written for men, deny and sublimate masculine desire.

The male body is thus troped and marginalized by Miller, Post, and others as the corpus of the provider, whose domain is the office and the cocktail party, the soda fountain, and the car seat. In seeming contrast, etiquette books by male authors provide an elaborate map to men's social desires and goals within the patriarchal world. The authors of these texts accept the diametric opposition between the feminine and the masculine, a "them versus us" strategy that leads to an (unnatural) separation of men and women and the separate spheres of female/private and male/public interests. Accordingly, the main selling points of etiquette books for men is the promise of an increase of social confidence and economic gain in the public sphere through manners. The grotesque body of the male is troped as a fiscal commodity, denied individuality, and constrained physically.

In conjunction with this, Victor Seidler argues in *Rediscovering Masculinity: Reason, Language and Sexuality* that the body of the male has been reared largely with such "a deep and unspoken investment in seeing [itself] as a 'rational being,' able to determine and control his life" that when this illusion (and it most assuredly is just that) is shattered, men "erupt and get speechlessly angry, even violent, in sustaining this image of ourselves" (62). Seidler sees men as conditioned to "use language to conceal our fear, dependency and vulnerability" (149) and masculinity as a discreet and changing "externally defined" set of roles, "an ideal that we are constantly struggling to aspire to . . . [noting the] deeper importance of work in men's lives, since it was through doing a 'man's job' that men could feel secure in their identity" (151). Thus, the male body is fragmented into a series of troped performance areas, divided into various social, political, and/or sexual functions. Indeed, one of the most destructive myths Seidler explores is that of sex as performance or conquest, "not as a matter of pleasuring and nourishing the body, but as an individual achievement . . . within the pecking order of masculinity" (39).

In other etiquette texts for males, fear of financial and social failure is typically exploited. *Manners for Moderns,* written in 1938 by Kathleen Black for an audience of very young men, asserts: "No one who wants to be a success in his social, family, or business life can afford to neglect his manners. . . . Using good manners is like putting money out at interest—you get back more than you put in" (7). Accordingly, *Corporate Etiquette,* a text composed in 1970 for the benefit of the young businessman, includes a metaphor for the performing executive, "whose dreams are not bound down to mundane paths, but who is eager to go up the gratifying escalator of managerial success" (Jarman xiv). These admonitions clearly can be seen as attempts to trope the male body in the area of public performance, and yet the private consequences of these restrictions would seem to be, as Seidler argues, fearfully oppressive for the conventionally socialized male.

In the language and tone with which women etiquette writers treat men, one is continually reminded that in the home, women are expected by Post and other authorities to set the rules and standards that operate within this separate sphere. Not only do women preside over Post's 1922 "Well-Appointed House," but they perform dominating rituals such as "Teas," "Balls," and other "Formal Dinners." Men are completely absent from Post's utopic vision of "Teas and Afternoon Parties," for example. Men are viewed as incompetent in the detail work involved in preparation for the formal dinner. In "How a Dinner can be Bungled," the central female character asks her husband, "What is the matter with the forks?" sensing something is wrong with the place settings. Something is entirely "wrong," but "he does not see anything wrong" (*Post's Etiquette* 180). The husband is of no use or help to the distressed wife undergoing a social failure. He does not even view it as such.

Male figures in Post's narratives are "problems" of etiquette in the home rather than helpmates. "Mr. Blank," for example, wreaks havoc to "Mrs. Gilding's" well-planned formal dinner when he telephones to say he cannot make it. "Mrs. Gilding" scrambles about until her butler saves the day by quickly thinking to telephone "Mr. Bachelor," who fills the "odd place." The domestic male who has been "with her for years" is of use to Mrs. Gilding, but the males of her stature are problems, performers objectified by Post in the narrative. The keenly chosen names of these figures demonstrates Post's ability to pigeonhole types of male figures, as they are labeled not by appearance but by what they have to offer the female sphere. "Mr. Blank," who so rudely calls to cancel, is indeed a "blank," a "zero" so to speak, of no use to "Mrs. Gilding." "Mr. Bachelor" is of use by virtue of his availability, which is stressed in importance by his name. He "favors" or performs for the hostess by "filling a space"; thus, he is objectified to the point of a chair occupier.

Men are ranked by importance in Post's section on seating and service. For example, in a chart designed for entertainment of a dinner of eight, the male figures are dubbed "1st Gentleman" and "2nd Gentleman" while their female counterparts are called "Lady of Most Importance," and "Lady" (*Etiquette* 206). "Gentlemen" and "Ladies" are ranked in

Post's order, and men are expected to submit to this performance system and support it by escorting the female of their "rank" into the room. Upon his arrival, the gentleman is given an envelope that tells him "the name of the lady he is to take to dinner." Post describes the exact size of such an envelope and adds to the formal importance by adding that they should be "arranged in two neat rows on a silver tray and put in the front hall."

The front hall is the physical and psychological entryway to the private sphere in the day of calling cards. It is a most important place in Post's world, where calling cards are exchanged and "well-bred" hostesses perform rituals. In "a certain few well-appointed houses," gentlemen are shown a table diagram when they enter the front hall. Significantly, gentlemen leave their hats and coats in the front hall. These outer accouterments are reminders and manifestations of their supremacy in the public sphere. As they enter the private sphere, they shed these symbols of power and submit to the female-dominated sphere. Immediately upon entering the drawing room, "a gentleman always falls behind his wife," writes Post, and the butler "announces the wife's name first," establishing the site of the female within the domestic sphere (*Etiquette* 213).

Men perform services that underscore women's primacy in hospitality. For example, "Mr. Oldname," the embodiment of established wealth, "always comes forward and, grasping your hand, accentuates his wife's more subtle but no less vivid welcome." Post directly alludes to the social primacy of the hostess, cautioning her not to "over-exploit" her guests with "embarrassing hyperbole." A poor hostess can overstep her warden-like status, forcing subjects upon her guest, "like a pair of manacles." The male guest is psychologically and corporeally subject to the whim of the hostess. An outdated convention, "The Turning of the Table," also underscored the dominance of the hostess. Here, the hostess performs the function of shifting discussions. She "merely turns to the gentleman (on her left, probably) with whom she has been talking with the soup and the fish course, to the one on her right" (*Etiquette* 217). Everyone at the table is expected to follow suit, turning to the opposite direction.

Most etiquette books for women, then, seemingly enforced a code of subjugation over the marginalized and fragmentized male, who is objectified as a performer of tasks within middle- and upper-class homes. However, it is important to note that this order exists only when the female hostess is in charge of performance tasks in the private sphere. Only occasionally would this schema be extended to the public/business sphere. Men, accustomed to troping their bodies as part of everyday commerce, maintained an inequitable "upper hand" in business affairs; indeed, the very act of possessing a male body was (and still in many instances is) seen as a prerequisite for "doing business" within the structure of American commerce. Since most business enterprise in the United States during the teens and twenties was largely governed and operated by men, women's power in the troping of the performative male in this instance would seem to be illusory and limited almost solely to the private sphere of the home.

The Victorian aestheticizing of the American etiquette book writer not only strengthens the symbolism supporting the family unit but also disguises the basic information by which mainstream society defines and marginalizes the other or anyone who does not support or maintain the patriarchal hegemony. Those on the outside of the boundaries of the working-class family, including people of color; "foreigners"; nonheterosexuals; non-Protestants; those seen as socially, psychologically, or physically impaired; and, to a lesser extent, even the extremely rich and the extremely poor are largely ignored by Emily Post, with the exception of domestics who are bodily troped as extensions of a proper (white) home.

Not surprisingly, few etiquette books have been written by and for African Americans. African Americans have been subject to an orally and physically transmitted code of behavior. Unsurprisingly, African American women were expected to adopt the sexist codes of behavior expected of their white sisters. Critic Annegret Ogden finds support for this view in the anonymous 1838 article "Colored Americans": "Employ yourself in household affairs. . . . Always appear flattered by the little kindnesses he does for you. . . . A wife may have more sense than her husband but she should never seem to know it" (46).

The scant literature of etiquette writing for African Americans reveals a good deal of double-voicedness, a mixture of bitter ironic subterfuge aimed at racism and a blatant attempt to change society by changing the behavior of African Americans. One example of such writing is *The Negro in Etiquette: A Novelty*, published in 1899 by E. M. Woods. The book originated as a lecture, "The Gospel of Civility," delivered at the Lincoln Institute at Jefferson City, Missouri. Woods dedicates the book to "my sainted mother, whose early teachings inspired my youthful heart to battle for the right; to the logical obliteration of 'lynch law and mob violence,' and to the unity of the North and South" (i). Woods's text is emblematic of the African American uplift movement. His first task, as he sees it, is to change the behavior and gestures of African Americans, especially toward white people. Woods's text is certainly problematic. He instructs African Americans to adopt the behavior of dominant whites. For example, he says that "among the many bad habits of our race which we must get rid of before we can acquire an easy, graceful gait, is shambling, or a shuffling, awkward walk—a kind of dragging the feet along" (29). The author finds the "Negro" sadly negligent in other areas, and he devotes chapters to such topics as "Why Colored Men Fail to Doff Their Hats to White Ladies," "Say 'Sir', Not 'Boss'," "Oiling the Hair," and the "ludicrous" "Cake Walk" (iii–iv). Of moving into white neighborhoods, Woods admonishes, "[L]et it be distinctly understood and everlastingly remembered that people of refinement don't go where they are not wanted, if they are aware of it" (147).

In the chapter entitled "The Black Man Honors the White Man," Woods clearly tropes the body of the African American as the student of the white man. This attitude of false modesty adopted by the African American toward the white man is equated by Woods with the accepted custom of respect for a teacher. "Why shouldn't the black man honor the white man? Didn't the white man make him what he is? Didn't the white man let into his benighted soul the first ray of enlightenment, education, and civilization? Isn't he still the Negro's great teacher and benefactor?" (Woods 137). This teacher/student model is further problematized by the engraving on the next page. A white male teacher stands on a platform, dramatically pointing with one hand to a mathematical equation on a blackboard. He holds a massive book in his other hand and looks down with stern patience at the unruly and confused group of African Americans who fill the classroom. The passage can be read as subversive political wit as well as straightforward correction.

At the back of the room, a group of African American women raise their hands to ask questions. These women perform theatrically the example of "correct" behavior. Sharing the stage with the white male teacher is the finely drawn figure of a white woman seated at a desk, looking directly at the African American women in the back of the room. Her presence, at least in terms of the image's narrative, seems unnecessary. Perhaps she could be seen as another teacher or a secretary to the male professor. She is presented as an iconograph representing white women as a group, who metaphorically share the same power base as white men. This white woman connects solely with the other women in the classroom; the African American male figures avoid her gaze, staring directly at the white man.

At the center of the group is an elderly African American male figure, who stands, stooping, lost in thought, as if trying desperately to understand the equation on the blackboard. This figure may represent a subversive performing body, a lone elder seer figure who subverts quietly the racism around him, perhaps even a representation of authorial subversion. Woods acknowledges his hope that time will change this white-supremacist model with the encouraging remark that "all this will naturally right itself when the Negro becomes a full-fledged universal teacher . . . [but for now] the White Man is to the Negro what the sun is to the earth—his light" (Woods 139). One cannot help but wonder at the double-voicedness of these passages which reveal subversive wit while not seeming to be overtly subversive. E. M. Woods reveals a brilliant ability to teach African Americans how to behave in a society that regards them as students that need "civilizing."

Sixty years later, in 1959, Stetson Kennedy challenged the racist social order with his book, *The Jim Crow Guide to the U.S.A.: The Laws, Customs and Etiquette Governing the Conduct of Nonwhites and Other Minorities as Second-Class Citizens.* Kennedy demonstrates that "ordinary rules don't apply to non-whites when it comes to etiquette." In his chapter "The Dictates of Racist Etiquette," Kennedy outlines the many no-win situations for even the most "mannerly" of Southern African Americans. He parodies the form of the etiquette book with his sections on such taboo subjects as "How to Avoid White Women," "How to Make an Interracial Introduction," "Handshaking Is Taboo," and "How to Talk Back and Live" (203–27). For Kennedy, the aestheticizing of the body of the African American was ultimately impossible. The nonwhite's outward appearance was a constant reminder to the Victorian-minded etiquette writer of his status as "other."

One of the main issues brought up by the absence of people of color in mainstream etiquette books is that race is treated as "a dangerous trope," to borrow Henry Louis Gates Jr.'s phrase (5). The trope is considered so dangerous that nonwhites are denied admission into the Edenic imagined paradise of writers such as Emily Post, except in illustrations showing the proper attire for one's servants. The humor in Kennedy's text is derived from this implausibility. Nonwhite people are a reminder of the Bakhtinian grotesque state that white conduct writers wish to deny.

Servants, who were often people of color, are often portrayed as grotesque and immoral in etiquette books. The hostess of the middle-class home is taught to fear the valet "Purloining little keepsakes from the portmanteaus of the visitors" (Crowninshield 117). Not surprisingly, we have evidence of how new immigrant domestic workers were treated from etiquette manuals. By 1900, "half of the 1.2 million maids, cooks, and charwomen had immigrant parents" (Ogden 121). These working women were viewed as "creatures to be pitied" (Ogden 126), but as we will see, "pitied" only from a comfortable distance. Emily Holt in her *Encyclopedia of Etiquette* of 1921 lays out the rules of etiquette between lady and servant: "Neither servant nor mistress profits by any lowering of the proper barriers set between them" (413). Discipline and emotive distancing were used as barriers between middle-class women and the grotesque servant/other.

Vogue's Book of Etiquette: Present-Day Customs of Social Intercourse with the Rules for Their Correct Observance, written in 1935, offers admonishments on the task of hiring a maid: "Beware of the talkative applicant! Servants who talk themselves into positions are generally the ones who talk themselves out" (139). Here, etiquette is called upon to do "that which [it] is primarily designed [to do] . . . to protect [or silence] one class from another" (Lynes 10). The example above also demonstrates the manner in which "difference" (aural or visual) is clearly felt as "an authorized trope for distinguishing between women" in the hierarchical struggle described by Kim F. Hall (10). As an immediately apparent iconographic aspect, racial difference often was used as a way of screening applicants with greater dispatch, no matter how inequitable the process might be. Further, hiring white women into white households strengthened the alignment of white women with the male class hierarchy.

Textual strategies for aesthetification were more subtle than the racist, sexist, and overtly homophobic pictorial illustrations one finds throughout etiquette books. Perhaps one of the most offensive examples can be found in *Manners for Moderns*. A young white male is reading a newspaper and having his shoes shined by a stereotypically drawn African American male, who is pictured with enormous, protruding lips. "Excuse me, Rastus, but do you mind if I read?" is the title under the illustration. A large question mark looms above the African American's head, to indicate his shock and surprise at this outburst of mannerly behavior being shown to a supposedly "socially inferior" person. A bold subtitle admonishes the reader to "Try Being Pleasant to Everyone for a Day." The text transforms the illustrative matter into a brutal display of the ruling hegemony. "Act interested in everybody. . . . Use all the good manners you have ever heard of on everyone from your closest friend to the corner bootblack" (Black 7).

Similarly, a backhanded reformer of 1940 wrote in favor of Southern (white) women beginning a movement to improve forms of social address toward African Americans. "Negroes, to be sure, are not the only creatures to whom we deny titles of respect, but about the only other human beings whom we so strip of their dignity and personality are prostitutes and prisoners" (Marion 638–39). Not only does this equation of African Americans with prostitutes and prisoners show how far down the social ladder African Americans were in American society during this period, but also it demonstrates that the underlying racist troping inherent in the social code of the time was comfortably overt, even to the casual observer. Marion's quote also shows how dangerous "loose" women (read prostitutes), unconstrained by codes of etiquette and chastity, could be to the existing social order. Further, by stating this equation, the writer may be unwittingly supporting the basic assumption upon which it is based: African American men and women are synonymous with prostitutes and prisoners. African American writers such as Frances E. W. Harper and many others challenged such racist assumptions.

Mainstream white etiquette texts, when demystified, betray a series of cultural artifacts in which the resistance to the performance of the aestheticized body is seemingly smoothed over, gilded, corseted, or desexed. The classical body is portrayed in an Edenic temple to the ruling female hostess, who only occasionally and temporarily submits to male authority. Men are ritually excluded from the design of the utopic female paradise, in which calling cards, deportment, cutlery, and above all, bodily management (as described by John F. Kasson) cushioned the family from the intrusions of industrial chaos, while it simultaneously fragmented the body into a dualistic model of distortion.

In this model, the classical body is constantly in fear that the mask of social performance will inadvertently drop to reveal the grotesque features of the performing body. Performance outside of domestic bliss was regarded with fear and revulsion. Masculinity, which was equated with rationality, had its flip side of otherness: as a sexual threat to the supremacy of the female, it would be sublimated and fragmented by the Victorian-minded etiquette writer. Gender roles were carefully outlined and separated, and nonwhites and members of the lower working class were either scarcely addressed or considered with scorn.

Etiquette and conduct writing has long been an area in which women writers have managed to exercise a writing and performing self. In the Middle Ages, Christine de Pizan wrote conduct texts not only for women but also for the knights and the highest members of the court (see Willard). Catherine Des Roches instructed the court in the sixteenth century on correct deportment (see Jones). Even Mary Wollstonecraft, who railed against notions of gender, prescribed domestic roles in her *Female Reader* (1789). As problematic as these texts stand to the feminist interpreter, they cannot be denied a place of importance: a stage for the relegation of the performing body in all its multivalencies, a stage on which some privileged women wrote their own oppressed version of femininity as they simultaneously seized the opportunity to become powerful social arbiters.

Though male writers held important roles as conduct authorities in earlier periods, women clearly staked out their primacy as etiquette writers by the end of the Victorian era, and they continue to influence and inform public social performance to the present day. Though many of the constraints of the body seen in *Emily Post's Etiquette: In Society, in Business, in Politics and at Home* may seem innocuous, they contain the roots of a system of oppression and self-denial inherent in controlling the display of the performing body as an act of social intercourse in Western society. Regardless of the gender or race of the author, etiquette texts stand as richly diverse sites for mining the cultural symbols of performance. Writers such as Emily Post succeeded in transforming the Edenic universe into a neatly decorated theater of performing anxiety, illustrated with place settings as oppressive to the spirit as they are pleasing to the symmetrically enforced eye.

2

The Knight's Body and the Female *Auctoritas:* Christine de Pizan's Conduct Texts

Much feminist criticism has drawn extensively upon Bakhtin's theories of dialogism and the carnivalesque, often in pursuit of a relationship between feminine authorship and dialogic discourse. Despite the problematics of appropriating a thinker who often did not include women in his discussions of literature, feminists have found Bakhtin's location of a "polyphony of the oppressed" (Herndl 19) useful in rereading the texts of women writers. Bakhtin's central preoccupation with literature as struggle is a useful feature to the feminist point of view. But how useful is Bakhtin to a study of a woman author who wrote, not from the oppressed margins, but as a member of the privileged medieval court?

Christine de Pizan ostensibly exemplifies, in her conduct literature, an ennobled writer for authoritative discourse. The problematics of approaching Christine's conduct literature from a feminist standpoint are heightened by her adoption of a seemingly monologic discourse, which attempts to control the unruly centrifugal forces of the grotesque body through the enforcement of centripetal rules of conduct. Nevertheless, I will argue that Christine used the parameters of authoritative discourse for a stage on which to display utterances of struggle against patriarchal homogeneity and authority. In a sense, my Bakhtinian reading of Christine's conduct writing challenges the criticisms of Bakhtin's binary categorizations as authoritative/nonauthoritative, monoglossic/heteroglossic, centrifugal/centripetal and privileges Bakhtin's polyglossic utterances, finding a hybridization of language and authority within the discourse of a female writer.

The hybrid construction I locate in Christine's authoritative conduct books demonstrates the limitations of Bakhtin's sharp delineation between authoritative discourse and internally persuasive discourse. Defined as an "utterance that belongs to a single speaker, one that actually contains mixed within it two utterances . . . two 'languages'" (Bakhtin, *Dialogic* 304), a "hybrid construction" breaches the gap between Bakhtin's binaristic categories. Though Bakhtin privileges the novel as the specific site of the hybrid construction, this method of "concealing another's speech" (305) can be detected even in the authoritative speech of the conduct text. For Bakhtin, "authoritative discourse," such as that of the clergy or state, reflects an "inertia" that bespeaks "its very nature incapable of being double-voiced; it cannot enter into hybrid constructions" (344). The authoritative word in Bakhtin's schema "is located in a distanced zone, organically connected with a past that is felt to be hierarchically higher. It is, so to speak, the word of the fathers" (342). Christine, by virtue of her gender and by virtue of her rhetorical ability, regenders the word of the father, dialogizing it to conform to an internally persuasive feminist dialectic, thus rendering Bakhtin's binaristic split between discourses as inapplicable. However, Christine's utterances, reread across a web of discourse of the languages of the father and the mother conform to Bakhtin's model of the heteroglossic. Christine's construction of herself as an *auctoritas*, through appropriation of the word of the father and dialogization of the word as a female, supports Bakhtin's view of language as "heteroglossic," wherein, "languages do not exclude each other, but rather intersect with each other" (*Dialogic* 291).

Christine's *auctoritas* arises not only out of her position as a female of the court but as an appropriator and compiler of the male word. Her texts display a network of resistances to the authoritative texts from which she borrows. Modern critics have mistakenly rejected Christine's conduct books for men as mere compilations of original source materials, as oddities on the periphery of her oeuvre. However, Christine's compilations of earlier male-authored conduct texts goes beyond mere legitimization. As a compilator, Christine "claims the traditional authority of her notable male auctores," notes Quilligan (*Allegory* 37). Christine's compilership has been viewed as a "position of power" (Blanchard 247), through which she legitimizes her undertaking. A tendency toward parodic heteroglossic utterances in which she exposes "cowardly reasoning, asides, parasitic argument, [and] long deliberations of questions" has been noted by Blanchard (246). Christine's figure of the *auctoritas*, then, is characterized as polyglossic, a speaker in many tongues. The discourse of her conduct books, far from being monologic, offers a feminist hybridization of homogenic authority.

After a discussion of Christine's dialogic display of feminine authority, I will examine her conduct books for men. In particular, I will examine the construction of the knight as a subordinated entity in the hands of a skilled *auctoritas*. Through the lens of a new historicist approach to the body and a feminist approach to the text, I will regender Bakhtin's grotesque model of the body as male. I am interested in the knight's body as a grotesque site of markings and power relationships and in the degree to which Christine's construction of authority and reconfiguration of the male body had cultural power beyond that which has been recognized through historical discourse. In this study, I am displacing notions of power as dominant hegemonic discursives and replacing a hermeneutic of heteroglossic power.

Christine recognized that "nothing is more material, physical, corporal, than the exercise of power" (Foucault, *Discipline* 58). Christine worked toward empowering her use of "women's language," as she actively defined models of conduct according to her desired gender order. While much criticism has been concerned with the construction of the feminine in Christine's conduct manuals for women, Christine's manuals for men stand as largely unexplored texts. Christine's chivalric conduct manuals offer a rare opportunity for a Bakhtinian examination of a site of discourse in which the female *auctoritas* exerts control over the male body. Christine's construction of the masculine, especially in the example of the knight, is a female-centered act, an act in which the hired knight is modeled to fit the standards of Christine's desired social order.

Christine's power over the male body was apparently considered specious and dangerous by translators and scribes of the period, who concealed her gender or, in some cases, even went so far as to regender her manuscripts. For example, some texts of *The Book of Fayttes of Armes and of Chyualrye* acknowledge Christine's authorship, while others exclude this fact. Even more provocative are the manuscripts of *Livre de faits d'armes*, which directly refer to the author as masculine, with all references to feminine authorship excised. Excised are sections of the first chapter, in which Christine invokes the traditionally employed modesty topos, seeks the aid and approval of the goddess Minerva, and ritually announces her gender and name. These careful regenderings support the need for a feminist reinterpretation of Christine's act of authorship and her authority over the male body.

Women writers and women mystics consistently have attempted to "write themselves," to exercise power even in the most oppressive and misogynist environments. Feminists and New Historicists have identified medieval mystic women's desire for "control of self" and explored the varying degrees of power they achieved through their mysticism and asceticism. It is not surprising, then, to find mystical texts by women that offer advice, often directed even at the clergy itself, for example, this piece by Mechtild of Magdeburg: "God knows, dear monk, you have been chosen for the highest . . . [so] you should be lovingly cheerful or gently serious with your subordinates and brothers and you should be compassionate regarding all their travail and with sweet words should you send them forth, preach boldly, and piously hear confession" (Wilson 177).

In an example of the feminine dialogic as a display of power, the same writer carefully crafts an indirect warning to the ruling clergy who have apparently not acted according to the demands of virtue. She sees them in "indescribable pain" in her visionary text "Heaven and Hell" (Wilson, 171–76). Mechtild and other women mystics such as Hrotsvit of Gandersheim were able to criticize the clergy and even exercise a limited degree of authority over the most influential figures of the church hierarchy because of their special status as sanctioned visionaries. Through their display of heteroglossic utterances, they both supported the orthodox church and its centripetal forces and subverted male authority through their centrifugal criticisms.

Christine became a conduct authority through her attachment to and patronage of the court of Charles V of France. Christine exercised a marked degree of authority on all levels of the court through her extensive writings in the area of conduct. These writings included *The Book of the City of Ladies* (1405) and its subsequent companion volume, *The Treasure of the City of Ladies* (1405), in which Christine created an allegorical city of outstanding women who embodied proper female behavior and provided extensive advice on female conduct in medieval society. In 1404, Christine composed *Le Livre des fais et bonnes meurs,* a manual describing her views on good government, written for Philip the Bold. *Le Livre du Corps de Policie* (1407) addresses the proper behavior of knights, princes, and other men. *The Book of Fayttes of Armes and of Chyualrye* (1410), Christine's conduct manual for knights, outlined proper moral and tactical wartime behavior. *The Morale Proverbes* (1400) is another example of Christine's extensive interest in codes of behavioral conduct between men and women.

The primacy of Christine's voice was established, then, through her writings on courtly behavior and her position within court society. However, Christine buttressed this power with an implied religious affinity to Divine Masculine Authority, as did the female mystics. In Christine's *The Book of the City of Ladies*, the allegorical female figure of Reason addresses the issue of women's authority:

> Similarly, God endowed women with the faculty of speech—may He be praised for it—for had He not done so, they would be speechless. But in refutation of what this proverb says (which someone, I don't know whom, invented deliberately to attack them), if women's language had been so blameworthy and of such *small authority* [emphasis mine] as some men argue, our Lord Jesus Christ would never

have deigned to wish that so worthy a mystery as His most gracious resurrection be first announced by a woman, just as He commanded the blessed Magdeline, to whom He first appeared on Easter, to report and announce it to His apostles and to Peter. Blessed God, may you be praised, who, among other infinite boons and favors which you have bestowed upon the feminine sex, desired that woman carry such lofty and worthy news! (28)

In the same text, Christine extends the domain of the female authorial voice, whose power is ascribed directly to God, to the domestic site of struggle between men and women. Lady Rectitude refutes the claim that "A MAN IS DESPICABLE WHO BELIEVES HIS WIVE'S ADVICE OR LENDS IT CREDENCE" (137). The texts of female conduct writers work to claim authority for women as social arbiters. Historians have largely ignored this arena of women's power, which allowed women the means of "organizing and directing ambition" (Curtin 423). The New Historicist reader looks for the erupting voice of the subaltern female, seeking to explore feminine constructions of authority and cultural power. In order to do this, one must suspend one's modern notions of feminism, in order to elucidate what might have been a medieval feminist agenda.

Christine, who attempted to "rewrite women good" (Delany 81) with her handbook for women, and to write men good, in her handbooks for men, supported a chivalric order that perpetuated sexism and sex roles, at least from a modern perspective. But there is a dialogic struggle for power in Christine's work, even as it seeks a new chivalric order "devoted to the defense of women's honor" (Willard 62–64). Christine's men were distinctly feminized through the careful use of heteroglossic strategies. Christine "feminizes valor and wisdom" (Chance 26) and "feminizes the mythographic tradition, valorizing the female" (123) in *Letter of Othea* and *The Book of the City of Ladies*. The text of the prologue to the *Letter of Othea* reads as a complex dialogic interaction between the body of the author, Christine, and the knight. Here, Christine presents the body of the feminized allegorical male, addressing Hector as "most high flower praised by the world, / to all pleasing and by God protected, / Gentle delight, sweet smelling, charming, / Of great worth, notable above all others" (1–4).

Juxtaposed with the humble prince or "noble flower" (5), Christine places her self bodily in the text with the feminine modesty topos, "I, poor creature, / unschooled woman, of small stature" (18, 19) and "I, named Christine, woman unworthy, / Have acquired knowledge, in order to undertake such worthy work" (54–55). Nevertheless, Christine uses centrifugal speech within an authoritative discourse to dehierarchicize the relationship of the sexes. She locates the bodies of Hector, Christine, and Isabeau as subordinate to the female body, which is "a thing spiritual and elevated above the earth; these are the images figuring in the clouds and the first one is the goddess of wisdom" (35).

Christine in effect claims authority over the body of herself, her reader and her allegorical figures in *Letter of Othea*. Quilligan describes this extraordinary feat, as it appears in the text of *The Book of the City of Ladies:* "Through the allegorical frame, she also stages her own authority . . . [and] she literalizes the gender that has been implicit in all female figures of auctoritas[,] itself a feminine noun that would require a female figure for its personification" ("Allegory" 233).

The dialogic discourse across gender lines between allegorical and real bodies subverts the conventional mirror topos typified in early conduct literature. Instead of the mirror of male auteur, Hector receives the look of a female sapiencia figure, a motherly deity who gazes lovingly, yet reprovingly, at her son, the reader, and/or Hector. This regendered authorial gaze is also at work on the male reader of *The Book of Fayttes*.

Christine evokes the *auctoritas* Minerva, the goddess of armor in book 1 of *The Book of Fayttes*. But first Christine characteristically postures her body humbly in the text, by invoking the modesty topos, a characteristic of her feminist dialogic:

> Seen the lytylhed of my persone / which I know not degne ne worthy to treate of so hye matere / ne durst not only thynke what blame hardynes causeth whan she is folyssh / I thenne nothyng moeved by arrogaunce in folyssh presumpcicion / but admonested of veray affeccion & good desyre of noble men in thoffice of armes. (11–17)

Christine's apostrophes invoke female *auctoritates*. Christine acts as her own compiler, invoking her heteroglossic utterances through the tongues of the figures of Wisdom, Minerva, Rectitude, and Reason. In calling to her writing self, the body of the *auctoritas* merges with the body of Christine, who has entered the text with a feigned posture of humility. The reader experiences Christine's heteroglossia at a dialogic crossroad between powerful *auctoritas* and submissive humble female:

> Adoured lady & hie goddess be though not displeased that I symple & lytle woman lyke as nothing unto the gretenes of thy renommee in cunnyng / dare presently compryse to speke of so magnyfike an office as is the office of armes. (10–14)

Christine again invokes the dialogic voice of feminine allegorical authority, Virtue, in the beginning of *Livre du Corps de Policie*: "O vertue, a thyng noble and deified, thoughe dar I be so bolde and avaunt myself to speke of the, whiche I know right weell that my vndirstondyng can not quckly comprehende ne vndirstonde clerly ne declare" (*Middle English* 15–18).

The modesty topos typically was used by both genders in the medieval period, but Christine seems to have employed the device in a manner that Julia Kristeva has termed the "language of gestures," which allows for signification of male and/or female roles that are "engendered before being fixed in the world" (*Language* 303–04). Ostensibly writing from a posture of submission to male authority, Christine employs the meta-linguistic device of gender mutability to appropriate power across the margins of gender. She freely compiles authority from both male and female authority figures, but she ultimately speaks as a woman writer. In *The Book of Fayttes*, Christine engages in authorial refraction of the male body, describing it in parts:

> [T]hat had a streyght hede a large brest / grete sholders & wel shapen armes & bygge & wel made / long handes & of grete bones small bely & the reynes wel formed / bygge thyes / leggis streyght wel shapen full of synewis & drye / brode fete & streyght / but as for the height of the body made noo force / and above al other thyng toke hede to the vigour and courage and to the swiftnes of the body / and to such yong men putte theyre mastres theyre besy cure & deligance to teche them the said arte & connyng of armes. (10–24)

This early example of female authorial control over the male corpus displays a manifestation of a monologic model of the idealized male. Foucault defines such a fragmentation of the body of a soldier wherein "the body is constituted as a part of a multisegmentary machine" (*Discipline* 164). Through Christine's verbal quartering and dismemberment of the male fleshly anatomy, the male body is objectified and fetishized. Through objectification, the conquered male body is thus reduced to a "fragment" of its corporeal being. This is not unlike the female fetishism found in the writing of George Sand (Schor 363–72).

Christine adopts the language of gestures of the prevailing patriarchal order, and regenders it with her pen/trowel. Well aware that the pen can be mightier than the sword, Christine eloquently reminds the male reader of her power as a social arbiter. Quoting Cato, Christine borrows and dialogizes the words of male authority and renders them as hybridizations of female authority:

> [T]he wrytyng of rules / techyngs and dyscyplyne of armes whiche he had composed & made in a boke / than in any thynge that he euer had doon wyth his body / for he saith all that euer that a man may doo / endureth not but one age / But that whiche is wreton endureth to the comyn prouffit ever more / by which Innumerable men may more a naylle / so is it thenne by this reason proued / that it is not a thynge of lytl prouffyt for to wryte & make bookes. (*The Book of Fayttes* 8–15)

In the passage above, Christine, through Cato, recognizes the power of writing books, especially conduct books, even beyond a historical period. Though this power is invested in "his" body, through the feminist dialogic, it is also invested in her body. Christine's quasi-direct speech across male authority characterizes internally persuasive discourse in Bakhtin's terms. However, Christine's use of the latter in the context of authoritative discourse of a conduct book merges the discourses that Bakhtin describes as oppositional. Nevertheless, Bakhtin locates this "process— experimenting by turning persuasive discourse into speaking persons," as a dynamic device in which "someone is trying to liberate himself . . . or is striving to expose the limitations of both image and discourse" (*Dialogic* 348). Here Christine exposes such limitations through her frequent use of the ennobled language of male texts, especially in *The Book of Fayttes*, in which she credits Vegetius, Frontinus, and Honore Bouvet, (Bouvet's *Tree of Battles*, a fourteenth-century military manual, was the major source of book 3 of Christine's manual). In the Caxton edition, Bouvet appears to Christine in a dream, essentially becoming at one with the body of Christine:

> As I dyde awayte for to entre in to the thirde partye of this present boke / & that my wyt / as almost wery of the pesaunt weyght of the labour concernying the two other partyes precedent / & as surprysed with slepe lyenge vpon my bed appiered byfore me the semblaunce of a creature hauyng the fourme of a stately man. (*The Book of Fayttes* 189)

In a stunning recognition of feminist dialogic authority, Christine uses quasi-direct speech to authorize herself. Christine ventriloquates through Bouvet, who offers his very tongue: "It is good that thou take and gadre of the tree of bataylles that is in my gardyn somme fruyte of which thou shalt vse" (189). Christine skillfully manipulates male authority when she mouths through Bouvet a statement designed to empower her as an able compiler. She says that "the more that a werke is wytnesed and approved of more folk / the more it is auctorysed and more auctentyke" (190). Bouvet is regendered into an *auctoritas*, who stamps Christine with authority: "for thy werke is gode / and I certyfe thee / that of many a wyse man hit shal be ryght well commended and praysed" (191).

Christine's dreamlike state, as Bouvet appears to her and makes a gift of his tongue, is reminiscent of an incident in the beginning of *The Book of the City of Ladies*, in which Christine falls asleep, only to be awakened by the three *auctoritates*. Through the medium of this convenient reverie, Christine injects her own grotesque body and its bodily functions into the text. Further, sleep becomes a fertile zone in which to ply her trade as a writer. Her "visions" are given credence through the feminist dialogization of male authorized speech. Her body is positioned in a power display not unlike that of medieval women mystics. Female authority is not limited to linguistic utterance in the conduct books of Christine. It is underscored and signified by illustrative matter, which adds a performative dimension to Christine's heteroglossic utterances.

Maureen Quilligan notes a "surprising representation of female authority" (*Allegory* 29), in a miniature from *Livre des fais d'armes et de chevalerie*. While Christine is depicted touching books in the incipits to her other texts, Christine does not touch the books, as Quilligan notes, in the chivalry manual. Instead, Christine gestures and looks at the female authorial figure, Minerva. Since Christine receives the information from the goddess, Quilligan argues, Christine "does not touch the books, as if there is no need to do so when the female authority (Minerva) is herself physically present" (29). Another interesting difference between the plates comes in the form of a bodily gesture of female empowerment. Christine stands in this plate, suggesting she is the authoritative equal of Minerva. Additionally, the two women *auctoritates* are slightly larger than the military men shown on the right hand side of the plate on horseback, seemingly awaiting orders from the feminine allegorical figures of authority.

Christine wished to have power over the grotesque and classical bodies of both men and women in the medieval French court and in society. She clearly desired that her chivalric conduct manuals would outlive her and continue to influence men's behavior as warriors and noblemen. Christine prayed for her posterity with these words:

> And yett I pray for a rewarde of theim that be lyving and their noble successours, the Kyng and othre prynces of Fraunce, that for remembrans of my sayinges in tyme to come whan the soul is oute of my body, to haue me in mynde in their devout prayers and devout orysons effred up by theim . . . like wyse I requyre knightis and noble men and all othre generally of what parte that euer they be of that heren or see this lytle wrytyng, that they will have [me] in their remembrans and for my rewarde that it wolde like theim to sey a pater nostur and an aue. (*Middle English* 25)

How much power Christine's "lytle writing" had over the knight's body is lost to history. Of more interest, I think, is an examination of this work with the nexus of cultural conscriptions of the male and female body. An examination of the body of the medieval knight conflicts with our modern notions of a hegemonic power structure of the masculine. The body of the knight was sequestered from some arenas of power. His actions were "closely circumscribed by the requirements of warfare" (Curtin 397). His actions were monitored and expected to support a military-based hierarchy. This power structure was designed, as was Christine's *The Book of the City of Ladies,* to maintain the protected status of the exalted feminine as kept and chaste, the modest virgin and wife. In support of this system of values, Christine advanced the notion that "through the practice of chastity women can become stronger and more independent" (Bornstein, *Lady* 29). The value of the male body was thus relied upon to secure the safety of the independent female corpus. The knight, as a direct consequence, relied upon the authoritative courtly system as a site of gender identification, much in the same way that modern sex roles are inculcated into adolescent males.

The medieval knight spent a good deal of time in battle, away from home, dependent upon a small group of aristocrats or the clergy for physical and emotional support. Indeed, the knight was marked by a physical blow to the neck, *the accolade*, which was administered by the objectifying lord as a physical manifestation of ownership. The masculine code of chivalry, invoked by Christine and other conduct writers and perpetuated to a large degree in courtly literature, depended upon the mercenary knight's submissive posture of obedience as low-other. The medieval outlook, which included the three estates of the body politic (as described in *The Body of Policy*), mirrored the dismembered male knight whose disunity precluded individuality, much less self-ownership of body or desire.

Theoretically, the medieval knight bodily supported the ecclesiastical establishment. The terms of chivalry served as reminders of the categorical denial of bodily pleasure and pain to both genders. The good knight turned over his body to a system of *differencing* and *cadency:* a series of officious rituals of ownership that included jousts, oaths, tests of obedience, strength, and loyalty. The wearing of the suit of armor constituted a denial of the probability of the death and harm to the body and symbolically deprivileged the body of its grotesque state by substituting flesh with an idealized (classical) mechanical body. As Katerina Clark and Michael Holquist note, "[S]ince the dominant ideology seeks to author the social order as a text, fixed, complete, and forever, carnival is a threat" (301). Ironically, the needs of state linked the knight with the carnivalesque disregard for mortality, thus, a conflicting set of messages were encoded in the discourse of knightly behavior.

Nevertheless, the denial of the grotesque body was such a prevalent topos that tales of the period reinforce the motif of an inviolate male corpus, incapable of being wounded. In this state of artificial grace, the knight cannot be wounded, in the same way that the mystics and seers of the period imagined themselves invulnerable to all methods of attack. The body, then, is metaphorically sealed; nothing comes in, and nothing goes out. Christine's knights embody this idealized trope: "[T]hey ought to be hardy, and that hardyness ought to be so ferme and constant that they ought [not] to flee [nor] parte fro bataille for feer of dethe ne for lkesyng of bloode ne lyfe for the wele of their prynce, for saue garde of the londe, and for the common wele, for and they do, they renne in the payne of lesyng of their hedes by sentence of the law and also shamed

for euer" (*Middle English* 123–24). The knight prepared for dismemberment and death in battle is held up by Christine as the ultimate symbol
of self-sacrifice. In the prologue of *The Treasure of the City of Ladies*,
Reason, Rectitude, and Justice wake Christine from the "propaganda of
laziness" with a call to arm herself once again with her pen: "The knight
who leaves the field of battle before the moment of victory is deeply
shamed, for the laurel wreath belongs to those who persevere. Now stand
up and make your hand ready, get up out of the ashes of indolence!" (31).

Christine's conduct texts display an attitude characteristic of the conduct genre, in which both men and women are encouraged to suppress
many of their carnivalesque bodily desires. Laziness and sleep, as seen
in the above passages, are manifestations of a loss of self-control, which
must be expunged from the body. Nor does Christine limit her domain
to the secular world. Bodily control is at the center of Christine's advice
to nuns. These women, exemplifications of the most extreme spectrum
of the classical de-sexed body, are told that "you must master even bodily
sleep and all your senses, . . . for even nature can be mastered and controlled by this virtue, that is, by a great desire to attain control over one's
body by the spirit" (*The Treasure of the City of Ladies* 140).

The suppression of the Bakhtinian-termed "grotesque" sexual body,
or the "quintessence of all fleshly evil," has been located in the body of
woman and the "low-Other" (Finke 443–44). The mercenary knight in
medieval society may be viewed as an example of the "grotesque" or
disposable body, who was encouraged by Christine and other conduct
writers to desire a "classical" body, a disciplined pleasure—denying body
co-opted by church and society. Christine deplored the boasting, sexually roaming, dishonest knight whom she warned ladies against: "[S]ee
how these men accuse you of so many vices in everything. Make liars of
them all by showing forth your virtue. . . . Remember dear ladies, how
these men call you frail, unserious and easily influenced but yet try hard,
using all kinds of strange and deceptive tricks to catch you, just as one
lays traps for wild animals. Flee, flee my ladies, and avoid their company—under these smiles are hidden deadly and painful poisons" (Quilligan, *Allegory* 256).

Christine's idealized knight was thus encouraged to denounce his
fleshly grotesque features and to aspire to a divine, inviolate corpus. Chapter 13 of *Livre du Corps de Policie* contains an outline of the "conditions"
of the "worthy man of arms." He must "hate all vice and flee from all
thyng vnsiittyng whiche be contrarie to noblesse, and that loue and sewe
all goodnes and good condicions" (Quilligan, *Allegory* 141).

Christine is most concerned with centrifugal language, or false utterances of men who employ the "right lewde vice of lyeng" (141). She
deplores those men who "call themself noble," but from "no true worde

cometh oute of their mouthe, nor in their promisses" (142). Christine even goes so far as to admonish ladies to "avoid too many [friendships] with men" because "when the men see that many frequent the place where they all would like to be received privately, they wickedly jump to conclusions and invent lies about one another" (*The Treasure of the City of Ladies* 115). Christine admonishes women to beware of those men who use flattery as a snare because their words metaphorically inflict violence on the body. She says that "his talk might as well drive a nail into the eye of the master or mistress; that is, he blinds him or her by his flatteries" (113). Christine's feminist dialogics continue to be reinforced by more contemporary female conduct writers. The feared male other, that grotesque embodiment of unfettered sexuality, is civilized in the decent twentieth-century gentleman, the successor of the knight in modern Western society. In the 1920s, Emily Post reminded the modern gentleman that his utterances must support the dominant social hierarchy: "The honor of the gentleman demands the inviolability of his word, and the incorruptibility of his principles; he is the descendant of the knight" (*Etiquette* 514).

Bodily control is still at the center of conduct expected of the twentieth-century civilized male: "[I]n his own self-control under difficult and dangerous circumstances, lies his chief ascendancy over others who impulsively betray every emotion which animates them" (Post, *Etiquette* 515).

The carnivalesque is at odds with the "utopian scheme of conduct manuals" (Flynn 73). Seen in this light, Christine's conduct manuals display a dialogic site struggle for bodily control. The body is at the center of a battle for definition among the needs of the state, the church, and the individual. In the fictive world of Christine, *The Book of the City of Ladies*, women *auctoritates* exist in web of power negotiations. In reality, Christine upheld the order of the ruling patriarchy, but she subverted its primacy in many displays of heteroglossia. Christine was all too aware that only a select few women of her time were women of authority, as she was. Christine herself was well aware of her status as a servant of the aristocracy, when she called herself "I, their servant" (*The Treasure of the City of Ladies* 180). Nevertheless, she hoped that her female-centered tracts would be "issued and spread among other women . . . and many valiant ladies and women of authority [would] see and hear [her advice] now and in time to come" (180).

In Christine's conduct manuals, the self-authorized *femme conduit* begins to "rewrite the violence against the female body" (Quilligan, "Allegory" 235). Christine influenced the history of desire in society through her conduct books, which upheld virtues that simultaneously exalted women and men who were trained to deny the grotesque body. The classical, rational chaste body could be viable only in the utopia of *The Book of the City of Ladies*, but Christine advanced the codes of chivalry as dominant precepts in medieval society.

Christine's conduct writing locates gender as a force beyond Bakhtin's definition of dialogism, using "another's speech in another's language, serving to express authorial intentions but in a refracted way" (*Dialogic* 324). Christine's discourse is also a hybridization of Bakhtin's model, in that it constantly exposes a woman thinking and writing in an authoritarian mode, while subverting that same authority in an early feminist discourse. This rereading of Bakhtin through the lens of the work of a female author breaks down the binarisms that many feminists find offensive in Bakhtin's writing and exposes their inherent mutability. Writing in a privileged authoritative discourse, Christine displaces male authority and exhibits linguistic and textual control over the male body. The body of the knight and the authority of the male *auctoritates* are deprivileged somatically to conform to the desires of a female, in so doing, firmly establishing a feminine dialogic. The body of the lady, through Christine's feminist agenda, rises above the status of low-other, both textually and extratextually. Christine's conduct texts problematize Bakhtin's model of authoritative discourse. Though they attempt to determine "the very basis of our behavior" (*Dialogic* 342), they display a network of female resistance. It is true that within authoritative discourse "it is considerably more difficult to incorporate semantic changes into such a discourse" (*Dialogic* 343). Christine injects a network of resisting heteroglossia into the ennobled discourse of the conduct book. Her dialogisms bring together authoritative discourse and internally persuasive discourse, forces that Bakhtin believed to be oppositional and exclusionary. By regendering male *auctoritates*, Christine goes beyond transmitting another's discourse. Though he does not specifically mention women writers, Bakhtin seems to have located the feminist politics of this schema, in which "[o]ne's own discourse and one's own voice, although born of another or dynamically stimulated by another, will sooner or later begin to liberate themselves from the authority of the other's discourse" (*Dialogic* 348).

3

Isabella Whitney and the Performative Poetics of Correction

The sixteenth century has been read as a historical moment in which the body was placed at the center of the struggle for social control. Georges Vigarello locates the sixteenth-century body as a performative vehicle that "mimics and adopts the positions required by decorum" (188–89). "A new court nobility was being established as the world of chivalry faded, and the emergence of formal etiquette and a courtier class seemed to generate rules of deportment for the body" (Vigarello 151). The popularity of *The Book of the Courtier*, by Castiglione, reflected the shift toward attention to the behavior of the nobility. The rules of etiquette were not simply a matter of refined table manners, but they extended to the code of the lover. Not only is Castiglione's male courtier expected to control his bodily performance, but his domain extends over the body of the female object:

> [T]he lover should honour, please and obey his lady, cherish her even more than himself, put her convenience and pleasure before his own, and love the beauty of her soul no less than that of her body. He should, therefore, be at pains to keep her from going astray and by his wise precepts and admonishments always seek to make her modest, temperate and truly chaste; and he must ensure that her thoughts are always pure and unsullied by any trace of evil. And thus, by sowing virtue in the garden of her lovely soul, he will gather the fruits of faultless behaviour and experience exquisite pleasure from their taste. And this will be the true engendering and expression of beauty in beauty, which some say is the purpose of love. In this manner, our courtier will be most pleasing to his lady, and she will always be submissive, charming and affable and as anxious to please him as she is to be loved by him; and the desires of both will be very pure

and harmonious, and consequently they will be perfectly happy. (Castiglione 335)

The performing body of the female was placed at the center of the gaze of the male conduct writer of the Renaissance. As Ann Rosalind Jones has noted, "women were consistently the objects of scrutiny and targets of complex prescriptions for proper behavior" (39). Castiglione's *courtier* reveals a hierarchical model of control of gendered bodies tied to utopic ideals of masculine and feminine "faultless behavior." Jones locates the "marketing manners" (63) of Isabella Whitney as "one exception to the rule of modest silence" (63). Certainly, other women writers of the period have been identified as subverting the primacy of the patriarchal Word of the Father, but Whitney is particularly important for her challenges to the role of the male conduct authority. Taking up the role of the conduct writer, Isabella Whitney, known as one of the first professional women poets of Britain, was a middle-class secular woman writer of the late sixteenth century. Whitney is especially important as an early woman writer who voices a performative poetics of control of the female body, and even more blatantly and suggestively, the male body. A dialogic erupts in the voice of this woman poet, who both supports and disrupts hegemonic concepts of conduct. Whitney's letter to an unconstant lover demonstrates a double-voiced discourse that is perhaps characteristic of courtesy literature. Courtesy literature constructs a polarization between the performing self and the Bakhtinian "grotesque" body, between the real and the utopic, or as Ullrich Langer defines, the split between the "specific and universal" (218). Langer elucidates an "unstable mixture" (228) found in courtesy literature, which is problematized and reflected, as I will note, in the words of Isabella Whitney. Langer reads Renaissance courtesy literature as a dialectic struggle

> between the description of an illustrious courtly ideal never fully incarnate and the establishment of a set of rules enabling courtly practice and prescription. These two intentions, one roughly Platonic and the other roughly Aristotelian, are in the end contradictory, for the more substantial the ideal becomes, the less can it accommodate varying experience and therefore practice. The impulse to set forth an ideal as something outside of variety through which experience is to be judged is incompatible with the production of that ideal through the experiential mean of varying extremes. (218)

In order to locate Isabella Whitney's poetry in the context of courtesy literature, it is necessary to look across texts from a new historic perspective. The labeling of texts into fragmented categories is a limiting practice that displaces the investigation of the history of the literature of the body from the performing body. Peter Stallybrass defines the study of the cultural notions of the body as an analysis beyond the scope of the "habits of the body" (123). Stallybrass emphasizes the importance of conduct: "To examine the body's formation is to trace the connections between politeness and politics" (123). The gendered bodies in the work of Isabella Whitney enact the contradictory intentions of a nexus of discourses anchored in rules of conduct of the historical period, the politics of gender, and the ambivalence of female authorship. Like Mary Sidney and Aemelia Lanyer, who Wendy Wall argues "write within and against an ideologically problematic discourse, revising the representation of the female body" ("Our Bodies" 53), Isabella Whitney presents the male body on display, subject to the female gaze of authority. Whitney's letter "To Her Unconstant Lover" folds Castiglione's precepts back upon male authority and the male body as she attempts to make him modest, temperate, and chaste through her dialogic of loving advice/scolding.

"The Copy of a Letter Lately Written in Meeter by a Yonge Gentilwoman: To Her Unconstant Lover" is a fertile display of female poetics, capable of reworking the popular lament of the male poet as a lament of the abandoned female, yet Whitney, as Ann Rosalind Jones points out, "deploys contemporary gender ideology in order to establish a profitably respectable speaking and writing position for herself. She echoes conduct-book commonplaces on the good wife in order to write her way out of the discursive double bind that positioned loquacious women as whores, on the one hand, or, in the case of Ovidian lament, as exemplary tragic victims" (65). It is remarkable how quickly Whitney dispenses with the good wife role to pick up that of the conduct writer. The poem begins with a dialogic admixture of admonition and advice:

To Her Unconstant Lover

As close as you your weding kept
    yet now the trueth I here:
Which you (ye[t] now) might me have told
    what nede you nay to swere?

You know I always wisht you wel
    so wyll I during lyfe:
But sith you shal a Husband be
    God send you a good wyfe.

And this (where so you shal become)
    full boldly may you boast;
That once you had as true a Love,
    as dwelt in any Coast.

                        (Woudhuysen 187)

The traditional amorous verse epistle, as defined by Richard Panofsky, has much in common with the ideological polemics of the persuasive conduct book: "As attempts by a persona to communicate an experience and at the same time to persuade another to a desired action, these epistles exercised the poet's ability to write rhetorically artful persuasions" (2). Whitney's persuasive poetic art is all the more polemic because she grounds her depiction of her own body in the vehicle of the abandoned woman in the utopic conduct model only to "displace the seductive artifice traditionally attributed to women onto deceptive men" (Jones 66). Whitney cites a host of classical male archetypes of male betrayal. Rewriting the male body as the underminer of constancy in marriage is a retort to a body of literature that includes a trenchant tradition of condemnatory discourses against women. The inclusion of classical heroines as exemplifications of virtuous female archetypes is a consistent trope characteristic of women conduct writers. The rewriting of Ovid's *Metamorphoses* is particularly important in both Isabella Whitney's letter and Christine de Pizan's *Cité des Dames*. As Maureen Quilligan notes of the latter, de Pizan enlists three Ovidian heroines, Medea, Thisbe, and Dido "in the forces of feminine constancy" (*Allegory* 174). Similarly, Whitney invokes Dido and Medea in praise of their moral constancy juxtaposed against male inconstancy:

> Example take by many a one
> whose falshood now is playne.
>
> As by *ENEAS* first of all,
> who dyd poore *DIDO* leave,
> Causing the Quene by his untrueth
> with Sword her hart to cleave.
>
> Also I finde that *THESEUS* did,
> is faithfull love forsake:
> Stealyng away within the night,
> before she dyd awake.
>
> *JASON* that came of noble race,
> two Ladies did begile:
> I muse how he durst shew his face,
> to them that knew his wife.
>
> For when he by *MEDEAS* arte,
> had got the Fleece of Gold
> And also had of her that time,
> al kynd of things he wolde.

> He toke his Ship and fled away
> regarding not the vowes:
> That he dyd make so faithfully,
> unto his loving Spowes.

(Woudhuysen 188)

Whitney may, as Betty Travitsky notes, "understand the passive role played by the subordinated female in the game of marriage" ("Wyll" 80), but she reclaims the subordinated body of the female much in the same manner of Christine de Pizan. Both writers hold up the martyrdom of Penelope as models of female correctness. Whitney emphasizes the constancy of Penelope's martyrdom in a section of the poem that bespeaks a feminine dialogic. Ostensibly, Whitney wishes the inconstant lover a wife of chasteness above that of Penelope and Thisbie, among others. However, Whitney is politely wishing the violent ends of Penelope and Thisbie upon this new wife, even as she laments in the courtly civil tongue required of the amorous love poem:

> But rather the[n] you shold have cause
> to wish this through your wyfe:
> I wysh to her, ere you her have,
> no more but losse of lyfe.
>
> For she that shal so happy be,
> of thee to be elect:
> I wish her vertues to be such,
> she nede not be suspect.
>
> I rather wish her *HELENS* face,
> then one of *HELENS* trade:
> With chastnes of *PENELOPE*
> the which did never fade.
>
> A *LUCRES* for her constancy,
> and Thisbie for her trueth:

(Woudhuysen 190)

Whitney elevates herself from the role of adviser to prophet with a reference to Cassandra. After reminding the inconstant lover of her fidelity, she implicitly warns him of the possibility of her prophetic power, even as she denies it. When the poet wishes the male figure "no worser than" she wishes herself, she metaphorically inflicts on him the pain and scorn of the betrayed lover:

> These words I do not spek, thinking
> from thy new Lover to turne thee:

Thou knowst by prof what I deserve
    I nede not to informe thee.

But let that passe: would God I had
    Cassandraes gift me lent:
Then either thy yll chaunce or mine
    my foresight might prevent.

But all in vayne for this I seeke,
    wishes may not attaine it
Therfore may hap to me what shall,
    and I cannot refraine it.

Wherfore I pray God be my guide
    and also thee defend:
No worser then I wish my selfe,
    untill thy lyfe shal end.

(Woudhuysen 190–91)

Next, Whitney speaks of the inconstant lover. Her references to Nestor's status, Xerxes's wealth and Cressus's gold place wealth and status below the moral and spiritual plane of faithfulness and marriage. Indeed, one might argue that Whitney damns her lover to a constancy in death:

And after that your soule may rest
    amongst the heavenly crew.

Therto I wish King Xerxis wealth,
    or els King Cressus Gould:
With as much rest and quietnesse
    as man may have on Mould.

(Woudhuysen 191)

His soul "may rest," "with as much rest and quietnesse / as man may have on Mould," but then again, there is the possibility that his soul will not find this peace.

Whitney's poem may be addressed to an individual, yet her allusions and techniques construct a wider audience of readership. As Jones notes of Whitney and Catherine Des Roches, another woman poet of the period: "These poets' negotiations of cultural prohibitions and permissions demonstrate that conduct books and women's lyrics occupied the same ideological terrain in the second half of the sixteenth century. The nets and bridles that restrained women's participation in literary culture also provided them with entries into it in ways that mentors of elite manners and Protestant preachers could hardly have foreseen" (67). As Elaine V.

Beilin notes, Whitney's letter goes beyond "advocacy for deceived women" (91). Whitney mouths a feminist prophecy for the immoral male. The male readership is chastised along with the subject of the poem. Whitney turns her feminine gaze to the reading male body, who is reminded that "betrayers of women in particular will suffer the 'perpetual Fame' or rather, 'shame' of being known as unfaithful lovers" (Beilin 92). That the woman speaker wishes the deceiving male "as much rest and quietnesse / as man may have on Mould" betrays a curious feminist dialogic twist in Whitney's choice of words. On the one hand, she wishes him, ostensibly, peace in death, but, on the other hand, she regenders the tradition of the male conduct writer, who silences women; Whitney silences men. Combining the voice of the scorned lover, the conduct poetess, and the female prophet, Whitney makes use of a heteroglossia. As defined by Mikhail Bakhtin, heteroglossia is "another's speech in another's language, serving to express authorial intentions but in a refracted way" (*Dialogic* 325). Though Bakhtin is unconcerned with locating a feminist or feminine dialogic, his notion of "double-voiced" or "polylogous" discourse serves to help deconstruct the gap between authorial intentions and authorial invention with "authoritative" or traditional discourse.

Heteroglossic speech, as it is displayed in Whitney's letter, conforms to Bakhtin's paradigm, in which it "serves two speakers at the same time and expresses simultaneously two different intentions: the direct intention of the character who is speaking, and the refracted intention of the character who is speaking" (*Dialogic* 324). In Whitney's poem, the voice of the scorned lover has an agenda, and the poet has an agenda. Whitney conforms to a traditional type of poem even as she uses it as a platform for female dialogism. Whitney is able to speak in an environment in which women were discouraged from speaking, but she is able to chastise, prophesize, and moralize as well, proving Bakhtin's thesis that "one's own discourse and one's own voice, although born of another or dynamically stimulated by another, will sooner or later begin to liberate themselves from the authority of the other's discourse" (*Dialogic* 348).

Isabella Whitney's inclusion of classical heroes and heroines is deliberately polemical. The references to the classical figures of Aeneas, Dido, and so forth, act to decenter the "enobled discourse" (Bakhtin, *Dialogic* 384) of the love poem. In ennobled discourse, Bakhtin writes, classical illusions, or other literary allusions, are "polemically set against the brute heteroglossia of the real world and painstakingly cleansed of all possible associations with crude life" (385).

Not so in Whitney's letter. Whitney's letter seems designed to welcome the puncturing of the illusion of a classical utopia, as it reminds the listener of brutal distance between the conduct of men and women and the expectations of behavior in authoritative discourse, such as the conduct book or the Word of God. The ennobled discourse of the conduct manual has been identified as a utopic model, one that "could only exist in an Edenic imagination" (Flynn 73). However, the poetic forms can be written as heterotopias, which, as Foucault notes, "are disturbing, probably because they secretly undermine language." However, as Foucault states, utopias such as conduct or courtesy books "afford consolation" (*Order* xviii). Whitney's authorial intent takes dialogic speech across the boundaries of utopia and heterotopia. While she embraces the model of behavior espoused in a utopic episteme of courtly behavior, she undermines language in her own charged dialogic utterances, expressing multiple authorial intentions. Her heterotopic is disturbing because it is difficult to disentangle from the utopic classical allusions. There is a certain degree of mutability in reading this poem. The poem breaks from the conciliatory model of the genre as Whitney marks the uncomfortable connection between politeness and personal politics across gender lines. Whitney's letter undermines the notion of a finite female body. The female body is in marriage dependent upon the fidelity and constancy of the male body. In patriarchal terms, she has no body, no language. Thus, when Foucault speaks of "man's experience" as a "body," Whitney's legacy questions Foucault's utopic notions as they are problematized by gender norms. Foucault's episteme articulates a body and a language: "[T]o man's experience a body has been given, a body which is his body—a fragment of ambiguous space, whose peculiar and irreducible spatiality is nevertheless articulated upon the space of things, . . . to this same experience, a language is given" (*Discipline* 314).

In the case of the Renaissance female writer, the body is not a given in terms of ownerships, nor is language a given. The female writer must take language, take her body and use whatever rhetorical skill and talent she has to rework the male Word in a female tradition. She must reclaim the female body, which is confiscated from her ontologically from a tradition of misogynist debate and a misogynist physical world. Whitney mixes moral platitudes with feminist subtexts in her collection of conduct poetry *A Sweet Nosegay*. As Elaine V. Beilin notes, Whitney adopts in *The Nosegay* the "role of teacher to men and women" (94).

The Nosegay is riddled with warnings of corruption that, as Wendy Wall notes, "pose a danger to the spiritual soul and the wandering book" ("Isabella Whitney" 48). In *The Nosegay*, Whitney's moral sayings are juxtaposed against the final poem, Whitney's will, which, Wall notes, was published shortly after the state began restricting women's ability to make a will. Wall reads *The Nosegay* as a "talisman to ward off—moral, physical, social and sexual danger" (48).

The moral proverbs that open *The Nosegay* partake in a dystopic view of a utopic behavioral model. Whitney inscribes herself bodily and textually as a female authority on conduct and does not limit herself to moral conduct.

The beginning of the poem announces Whitney's feminist intentions in a dialogic between a modesty topos of sorts (illness) and an appeal for women's self-education:

A Sweet Nosegay

The Auctor to the Reader,
This harvest tyme, I harvestlesse,
   and serviceless also:
And subject unto sicknesse, that
   abrode I could not go.
Had leasure good, (though learning lackt)
   some study to apply:
To reade such Bookes, wherby I thought
   my selfe to edyfye.

(Travitsky, Paradise 120)

Whitney asks for respect from the author, even as she couches herself in a topos of female humility:

And now I have a Nosegay got,
   that would be passing rare:
Yf that to sort the same aright,
   weare lotted to my share.
But in a bundle as they bee,
   (good reader them accept:)
It is the gever: not the guift,
   thou oughtest to respect,
And for thy health, not for they eye,
   did this Posye frame:

(Travitsky, Paradise 120)

Whitney espouses the cultivation of knowledge for women as a form of chastity and protection from danger:

Of worldly things, the chiefest is seld,
   a well contented mind:
That doth dispise for to aspyre,
   nor gapeth gifts to fynde.
   A soveraigne receyt.
The Juce of all these Flowers take,
   and make thee a conserve:
And use it firste and laste: and it
   wyll safely thee preserve.

(Travitsky, Paradise 122)

The Nosegay includes a special verse epistle to women in which Whitney inscribes in the female the need to control her performing body in her daily duties. In Whitney's schema, the Renaissance female's behavioral code is designed to protect her from earthly men and to please God:

An Order Prescribed by Is. W. to Two of Her Younger Sisters Serving in London

Good sisters mine, when I shal further from you dwell:
Peruse these lines, observe the rules
which in the same I tell.
So shal you wealth posses,
   and quietnesse of mynde:
And al your friends to se the same:
a treble joy shall fynde.
In mornings when you ryse,
   forget not to commende:
Your selves to God, beseeching him
   from dangers to defende.
Your soules and boddies both,
   your Parents and your friends:
Your teachers and your governers
   so pray you that your ends,
May be in such a sort,
   as God may pleased bee:
To live, to dye, to dye to live,
With him eternally.

(Travitsky, *Paradise* 122)

Whitney espouses sisterhood in this poem and associated sisterhood with protection against dangers both spiritual and physical:

Your Masters gon to Bed,
   your Mistresses at rest.
Their Daughters all do hast above
   to get themselves undrest.
See that their Plate be safe,
   and that no Spoone do lacke,
See Dores & Windowes bolted fast
   for feare of any wrack.
Then help yf needs ther bee,
   to doo some housholde things
Yf not to bed, referring you,
   unto the heavenly king.
Forgettyng not to pray

> as I before you taught;
> And geveing thanks for al that he
> hath ever for you wrought.

(Travitsky, Paradise 123)

Another verse epistle from *The Nosegay*, written by Whitney to one of her sisters, is not only an inscription of sisterhood but an interesting view of the female poet's anxiety about the role of writing as opposed to traditional female behavior:

> Good Sister so I you commend,
>   to him that made us all:
> I know you huswyfery intend,
>   though I to writing fall:
> Wherfore no longer shal you stay,
> From businesse, that profit may.
>
> Had I a husband, or a house,
>   and all that longes therto
> My selfe could frame about to rouse
>   as other women doo:
> But til some houshold cares mee tye,
> My bookes and Pen I wyll apply.

(Travitsky, Paradise 124)

Elaine V. Beilin comments on the "self-consciousness" of the poet and reads in the passage an "implied deprecation of her literary endeavors" (89), yet a dialogic reading allows for another reading of the poem. Perhaps Whitney stresses the point that she "could frame about to rouse / as other women doo" in a bragging manner. Subtextually, Whitney could be emphasizing her virtuosity. She could be just as good a housewife as she is a writer. Provocatively, Whitney never says her sisters could just as easily take up the occupation of writer. Though Beilin concedes that Whitney may have gained some "private satisfaction" from her role as moralist, Whitney's dialogisms suggest an understated public avowal of pride and satisfaction in her role as writer.

Indeed, Whitney puts down the role of housewife in "An Admonition . . . to All you Gentilwomen." As Betty Travitsky observes, "Whitney compares herself to a fish lucky enough to escape the hook, who has thereby learned to beware of snares" ("Lady" 262). Whitney's moralisms uphold the patriarchal hegemony of middle-class Protestant faith, yet her dialogisms betray a feminist stance toward a society in which women were often "undefended by family structure, working away from home [and] who had to abide carefully by the restrictions of their virtue" (Beilin 88).

Whitney is important as an example of an early feminist reformer who understood the political implications of the female underclass. Travitsky credits Whitney as one of the first women writers who "initiated the woman's voice in poetic protest" ("Lady" 283).

Isabella Whitney's role as social arbiter or moralist should be connected to that of the woman prophet. Early women conduct writers and early women prophets share a desire to control their own bodies and to extend that control over the body of the male authority. She makes specific allusions to her own public speech and her ability to think at the outset of her "Wyll and Testament":

> I whole in body, and in minde,
>   but very weake in Purse:
> Doo make, and write my Testament
>   for feare it wyll be wurse.
> And fyrst I wholy doo commend,
>   my Soule and Body eke:
> To God the Father and the Son,
>   as long as I can speake.
> And after speach: my Soule to hym,
>   and Body to the Grave
> Tyll time that all shall rise agayne,
>   their Judgement for to have.
> And then I hope they both shall meete,
>   to dwell for aye in joye:
> Whereas I trust to see my Friends
>   releast, from all annoy.
> Thus have you heard touching my soule,
>   and body what I meane:
> I trust you all wyll witnes beare,
>   I have a stedfast brayne.
>
> (Travitsky, "Wyll" 84)

Just as the female prophets stressed the importance of the witnessing of their prophesy, Whitney implores God and the reader to witness her "stedfast brayne." She defines her life not as long as her body lives but as long as she can speak. Only "after speach" does she will her soul to "hym." This stunning example of an early woman writers' self-inscription displaces her material poverty with plenitude. Wendy Wall sees the "Wyll" as a triumphant rewriting of the role of the poverty-stricken, abandoned woman who "transforms loss into a means of empowerment" ("Isabella Whitney" 56). The "Wyll" lists property that the speaker has been denied, thus taking issue with women's rights to goods as well as male ownership of earthly goods. Wendy Wall explains:

> Whitney reinforces a tradition tied to women's contested testamen-
> tary rights. The OED lists one of the definitions of "will" as "the
> desire to do something when the power is lacking." The formation
> of the female "will" in non-legal texts (fictional forms and advice
> books) is bound up both with the "wylling mine" of Renaissance
> women (their desires as speaking subjects) and with those restrictions
> that prevented their wills from being known. Whitney draws upon
> the threat posed by, and legal circumscription placed upon, female
> testators as a means of articulating her ambiguous relationship to
> the forms of public writing. ("Isabella Whitney" 55)

Whitney ties her gifts to the memory of her "wylling minde," as if to set
up a reciprocal relationship between the poet and the reader:

> And now let mee dispose such things,
>   as I shal leave behinde:
> That those which shall receave the same,
>   may know my wylling minde.
> I first of all to London leave
>   because I there was bred:
> Brave buildyngs rare, of Churches store,
>   and Pauls to the head.
>
> (Travitsky, "Wyll" 84–85)

Whitney's "Brave buildyngs" are reminiscent of the female architecture
established in Christine de Pizan's *Cité des Dames*. Both women writers
regender the world as a female city effectively appropriating material
wealth in a feminist display of subversion. Whitney reallocates wealth to
poor women:

> For Maydens poore, I Widdoers ritch,
>   do leave, that oft shall dote:
> And by that meanes shal mary them,
>   to set the Girles aflote.
>
> (Travitsky, "Wyll" 91)

Whitney's allocations to the poor once again have strings attached to the
poet's memory:

> And that the poore, when I am gone,
>   have cause for me to pray.
> I wyll to prisons portions leave,
>   what though but very small:
> Yet that they may remember me,
>   occasion be it shall:
>
> (Travitsky, "Wyll" 89)

Whitney continues to inscribe her memory in her own epitaph:

> And though I nothing named have,
>   to bury mee withall:
> Consider that above the ground,
>   annoyance bee I shall.
>
> (Travitsky, "Wyll" 93)

By the end of the "Wyll," Whitney drops the playful allusions to herself as an annoying bee/poet, and returns to the reality of her impoverished circumstances:

> To all that aske what end I made,
>   and how I went away:
> Thou answer maist: like those which heere,
>   no longer tary may.
> And unto all that wysh mee well,
>   or rue that I am gon:
> Doo me comend, and bid them cease
>   my absence for to mone.
> And tell them further, if they wolde,
>   my presence styll have had:
> They should have sought to mend my luck;
>   which ever was too bad.
>
> (Travitsky, "Wyll" 94)

Whitney's self-lament bespeaks a feminine dialogic at work. She wishes on those who miss her a guilt-ridden existence. Indeed, she would still be alive, were it not for their inability to mend her luck. Yet Whitney couches her utterances in the expected modesty topos of the will. Whitney's language is cast in the form of the heterotopia outlined by Foucault. Her ability to undermine authoritative language and form is characteristic of the centrifugal language that serves to undermine the unitary language of the patriarchal Word of the Father. Intersecting in Whitney's every utterance is the web of a feminist heteroglossia. As Bakhtin states: "Alongside the centripetal forces, the centrifugal forces of language carry on their uninterrupted work, alongside verbal-ideological centralization and unification, the uninterrupted processes of decentralization and disunification go forward" (*Dialogic* 272). Because all language is dialogized, it is impossible to reduce the words of Isabella Whitney to binaristic categories such as centripetal and centrifugal. As Herndl suggests: "In feminine texts it is never clear who speaks, where the speaking is coming from, but it is clear that there is always more than one speaker, more than one language because it is always 'an-others' speech, serving 'an-others' language. A feminine language lives on the boundary" (11).

I have tried to decenter Whitney's texts from the boundary between poetic and courtesy text. I have read Whitney against the backdrop of the male courtier of courtiers—Castiglione—in order to provide a backdrop on which to foreground the words of the female conduct poet. The woman writer as advice giver or prophet is a problematic power construct given the fact that "[i]n the ritualized practice of civility and etiquette, women would become . . . the representatives and the police of civilization's colonized desires, both Nature and Nurture" (Correll 652). Even as judging other, women such as Isabella Whitney served to reinforce the hegemony of patriarchal order and Christian codes of gendered behavior, but her every utterance is charged with a feminist performative of correction, one that begins to reclaim the female body and the female Word.

4

The Dialogics of Sisterly Advice: Hannah Webster Foster, *The Boarding School*

By writing her self, woman will return to the body
which has been more than confiscated from her.
                —Hélène Cixous, "The Laugh of the Medusa"

In "The Gendered Meanings of Virtue in Revolutionary America," Ruth H. Bloch provides an account of the "transition toward the personal and feminine definition of 'virtue'" during the American Revolution (38). Bloch traces the evolution of conceptions of "public" virtue from its definition as a masculine trait to its transformation in the Revolution. Ironically, as Bloch explains, "[t]he transformation in the meaning of virtue during the Revolutionary period sharpened the social boundaries between the sexes in ways that continue to deny power to all classes of women" (38).

Early American conduct texts exemplify the struggle for power over the female body. Though a body of critical studies in the area of conduct literature exists (Armstrong and Tennenhouse, Foster, and Sarah Emily Newton, and others), the intersection between the realm of the fictive narrative and the conduct manual needs to be more fully explored. In the dialogic struggle between the conduct manual and the newly crafted world of American fiction, one finds in *The Boarding School*, by Hannah Webster Foster, an example of the increasingly fluid boundaries contained within women's literature of the period. While *The Boarding School* presents itself to the reader as a fictional narrative, encoded within the diegesis of the text is a series of questions, yet also affirmations, of the standards and mores of Webster's world.

This creates a feminist dialogism, a fluid state in which Foster seemingly supports the standards of female virtue, while she simultaneously calls these standards into question. However, Janet Wilson James sees early women conduct authors as adherents to male standards of virtue and propriety, and she cites Hannah Webster Foster's *Boarding School* (1798) as a case in point (238–39). The *Boarding School* does not support this paradigm. In the first half of this epistolary novel, which takes the form of a valedictory address of a preceptress to her pupils, the narrator praises the domestic virtues: "piety, morality benevolence, prudence and economy. . . . 'Nothing lovelier can be found in woman, than to study household good'" (7). The dominant voice would seem to adhere to patriarchal constructs of virtue and deny the female public construction of self. The second half of *The Boarding School* consists of "A Collection of LETTERS, written by the Pupils, to their INSTRUCTOR, their FRIENDS, and each other." In this section, women speak to themselves in a manner that suggests a distinctive urge to create a new sense of the female self in a society dedicated to suppressing the female body.

Claire C. Pettengill scrutinizes the ambiguity of Foster's *Boarding School* in her study, "Sisterhood in a Separate Sphere: Female Friendship in Hannah Webster Foster's *The Coquette* and *The Boarding School*." Pettengill correctly ascertains that *The Boarding School* combines the hegemonic ideology of the conduct book with the subversive capabilities of the novel. In this light, Pettengill explains, *The Boarding School* is "able to bridge cultural contradictions in an effective way" (189). While I agree with Pettengill's placement of *The Boarding School* as a bridge between discourses, my reading locates it as more subversive than "moderate."

Toril Moi asserts that the critical tendency to seek out "integrity and totality as an ideal for women's writing can be criticized as a patriarchal or—more accurately—a phallic construct" (66). The denial of the possibility of subversive authorial intent within women's texts, which, on first glance, seem to be simply patriarchal tracts, has been questioned by new feminist criticisms. In this study, I will examine the manner in which Hannah Webster Foster uses dialogism, as located by Bakhtin: the use of "another's speech in another's language, serving to express authorial intentions but in a retracked way" (*Dialogic* 324), to explore the possibility of sisterhood in early America. These dialogisms represent conflicts between permissible and impermissible desires and are further complicated by the use of the "polyvocal" or "patchwork" narrative, a subversive form of narrative described by Josephine Donovan as one that, in early female texts, "fractured the authoritative, monologic modes of earlier patriarchal forms . . . and established the dialogic, ironic mode characteristic of the novel" (462). A close textual analysis of *The Boarding School* reveals a decidedly subversive tone and disrupts the world view in which nothing lovelier can be found in woman than to study household good. Like Foster's more well known novel, *The Coquette*, in which Sharon Harris finds a sisterhood of "women acting in consort, as a community separate from, and in opposition to, the oppression of the patriarchal republic" (15), *The Boarding School*, in many ways, explores the possibility of female community beyond household ornamentation.

In 1722, Cotton Mather lauded women as "People, who make no Noise at all in the World; people hardly Known to be in the World; persons of the Female Sex" (*Ornaments* 34, 35). Foster's preceptress only stands as an obvious exemplification of a woman who speaks (for the first 113 pages). Her address, in fact, takes a week in its entirety, and the collective response of the students reads as an audible song of female friendship and solidarity. These pupils make noise in the world, as their later letters will testify. The voices of the students "all united in testifying the sense they entertained of the advantage they had received from Mrs. William's tuition, the happiness they had enjoyed in each other's society, and their determination to remember her counsels, cultivate continued friendship among themselves, and endeavor to be worthy of hers" (113). The women of Harmony-Grove, a utopic sphere of female community, speak often and loudly, especially as they mature into activists and critics. The preceptress effectively "engraves" her voice on their memories (15), as she has set out to speak herself and their collective response seals a bloodbond of unity of women who speak.

Among the pupils of *The Boarding School*, Laura Guilford stands as one loud voice calling for speech among women. In her verse, Guilford proclaims:

> Thoughts shut up, want air . . .
> Speech ventilates our intellectual fire;
> Speech burnishes our mental magazine;
> Brightens for ornament, and whets for use.
>
> (174)

Matilda Fielding responds to Laura's letter with a recounting of a women's meeting in which she boasts the women found they could speak "without restraint, or the fear of criticism" (176). A letter from Amelia Parr interrupts the dialogue of the pupils of Harmony-Grove. In a strangely imperious tone, Amelia accuses Harriot Henly of having "strange ideas of the world," which she blames on the environment of the boarding school. Harriot responds with a cutting retort to her letter, saying that "your letter—your rattle, rather, came to hand today" (157). For Foster, Amelia represents the embodiment of the ornamental female, a body that is both critiqued and catalogued in the text of her work. Foster's attitude toward the ornamental female is one of contempt and ridicule, both in *The Boarding School* and in *The Coquette*. Foster does extend some sympathy toward patriarchally defined women such as Amelia, whom she views as constructs of a male-defined education system. Even as Foster voices her disgust with women like Amelia, she employs the dialogics of the novel-conduct book to criticize the era's patriarchally defined education of women.

Harriot Henly dismisses Amelia's criticisms of Harmony Grove, which she praises as a place where "we have no card-parties, avowedly formed for the purpose of *killing time!*" (158). The need for a sphere in which women could speak and study freely is a consistent subtext of *The Boarding School,* which was written at a time in which rhetoric against female boarding schools emphasized their supposed "undomestication" of women. In 1795, the Reverend John Bennett attacked boarding schools on the basis that they discouraged domestification of the female body, whose finest qualities were, for Bennett, "innocence, simplicity and domestick worth" (109):

> Boarding schools wholly counteract these dispositions. They trample upon nature, and give us artificial creatures, artificial looks, and artificial smiles. In their formal walls, airs, gestures, syllables, articulation, all are studied, and are sure to disgust. Like hot beds, they give a forwardness to the fruits, but deprive them of their natural healthiness and flavour; and the fine ladies they send into the world, feel themselves ridiculously exalted above (what they conceive to be) the groveling offices of family economy, or domestick attentions. (109)

An exchange of letters between Sophia Manchester and Maria Williams displays a characteristic voicing of support for the female boarding school. "Restore me again to the native simplicity and sincerity of Harmony Grove!" (H. Foster 149), writes Sophia, after criticizing the uneducated, overdressed women she finds in her new circle. "How vain then is this subterfuge?" she asks. "Beauty cannot possibly maintain its sway over its obsequious votaries, unless the manners and the mind unitedly contribute to secure it" (148). Matilda Fielding responds with an admonishment designed to defend women: "Few, you should remember, have had the advantages which you have enjoyed. . . . Let charity then draw a veil over the foibles of others, and candour induce you to look on the best and brightest side" (150). Education itself is consistently praised in highly embellished, almost hyperbolic metaphors of female pleasure. Julia Greenfield and Cleora Partridge, for example, decide to read geography tests together. Julia implores Cleora in a tone of romantic sublime: "Come, then, my dear Cleora, and without fatigue or expense, we will make a tour of the globe together. . . . We will traverse the frozen wastes of the frigid zones, and the burning sands of the equatorial region; then return and bless the temperate and happy medium in which we are placed" (226).

The rhetoric of *The Boarding School* not only actively supports the role of the education of women, but it provides a glimpse of early American feminist literary criticism. Sophia Manchester, for example, dismisses

Tristram Shandy, dismisses the "obscene and vulgar ideas" of Swift (205), and proclaims her preference for the history of women. Immersed in a text of American biography, she notes that "the native virtues of our sex suddenly reanimate our frame" (207), and she shows decidedly more interest in Isabella than Columbus and in Pocahontas than Captain Smith. Laura Guilford is another budding literary critic. "I am not equally pleased with all Richardson's writings" (161), writes Guilford, not missing an opportunity to criticize the male novel: "it dissipates the mind" (162). Pope's letters are artfully criticized by Caroline Littleton: "He, said I to myself, who bears the palm from all contemporary poets, and who is so consummate a master of this divine art, must surely furnish a source of superior entertainment. . . . The greater part of them have little other merit than what arises from the style" (126).

Both American and British conduct literature written by women often contains a surprising amount of literary criticism, with an even more surprising and enlightening feminist tone. Jane West's seemingly conservative *Letters to a Young Lady* (London, 1806) not only spends hundreds of pages criticizing Scripture, but it claims that, among Gothic romances, "only female genius can urge any pretensions to success (454), specifically in reference to Radcliffe's "fine Gothic romance of Otronto" (454). Indeed, for Hannah Webster Foster, as well as Jane West, the selection of reading materials, in a feminist canon making, takes the form of emphatic rhetoric which supersedes that of selection of husbands. Dr. John Gregory's *Father's Legacy to His Daughters* (1774) articulates the male conduct writer's emphasis on selection of husbands: "As I look on your choice of a husband to be of the greatest consequence to your happiness, I hope you will make it with the utmost circumspection" (126).

Hannah Webster Foster emphasizes the scrutiny of reading materials far more often than the scrutiny of perspective husbands. Novels "are the most dangerous kind of reading, now adopted by the generality of young ladies," warns Foster, adding that "their romantic pictures of love, beauty, and magnificence, fill the imagination with ideas which lead to impure desires" (18). Foster urges her pupils to read good poetry, essays, and in a display of self-reflexivity, epistolary conduct books. Foster even encourages women to write epistolary novels, couching her feminist rhetoric in patriotic language: "Thrice blessed are we, the happy daughters of this land of liberty, where the female mind is unshackled by the restraints of tyrannical custom, which in many other regions confines the exertions of genius to the usurped powers of lordly man!" (31). Foster embraced the power of the pen to reclaim the female body, and she understood its ability to span the course of time. "Always employ your pens upon something useful and refined," she wrote, adding the sage's wisdom: "'I am writing for futurity'" (33). On the choice of husbands, Foster provides ample advice, but she does this in a decidedly feminist manner. In *The Boarding School,* as in *The Coquette,* Foster warns her female audience: "'That reformed rakes make the best husbands,' is a common, and I am sorry to say, a too generally received maxim" (103).

Foster stresses the importance of relying upon female friendship and maternal guidance in matters of the heart. In one of the many allegories presented in the valedictory address, Florinda "saves" her friend Narciffa from an attachment "to a man who was much her inferior" (94). The women exemplify "the bonds of true and generous friendship" (94), and Florinda stops her friend from eloping by threatening to tell her parents. Foster stresses sisterly compassion and action in many of the allegories weaved into the patchwork of *The Boarding School.* Prudelia saves her sister, Myra, from ruin: when she hears that she has been seduced and abandoned. Prudelia gives up her lifestyle of affluence to seek out her sister and helps her to reestablish herself, and reclaim her virtue. The subtext here implies that even the most "fallen" women can be saved through sisterhood: "[T]aking her reclaimed sister with her, she returned to her anxiously expecting family" (88). Prudelia is acting upon the words of the preceptress, whose final remarks in the novel stress the ideology of sisterhood: "Watch over your dear little sisters, with all the tenderness of fraternal affection; be their protector and friend; instil into their minds the principles of virtue and religion; arm them against the snares and temptations by which they will be surrounded; and lead them, by your own conduct, in the way of truth and peace" (251–52).

In Hannah Webster Foster's ideological framework, for a woman to be praised is for her to act in union with her sisters. In Cotton Mather's *Ornaments for the Daughters of Zion,* "for a woman to be praised, is for her to be married" (32). Foster breaks with the traditional view, then, of women as chattel and redefines the female body as an empowered vehicle of female friendship. Foster views marriage as less of a choice than a proscribement. In fact, her most favored status for women seems to be the single female. Further, Foster suggests that the optimum status for a woman in patriarchal early America is that of the married woman whose husband is conveniently abroad! "Look upon Elvira," urges the preceptress: "Her acquirements in a single state have qualified her for a shining pattern of matronal duties. Her husband's business abroad prevents him from attending to domestic avocations; nor need he be anxious respecting the management of household affairs" (27). The preceptress ends her complimentary incantation on the merits of Elvira's household situation with a telling remark: "But I flatter myself that each of you, my dear pupils, will be an Elvira" (28). One cannot but think that Foster's subtext here would read "Be an Elvira." In a disruption of the patriarchal order, Elvira enjoys the privilege of the economic support of the patriarchy without its bodily restraints. She is free to read, write, and enjoy sisterhood. She stands as a model of the capable female; capable in both spheres, she creates her own sphere of empowered status. Jane West, Foster's British counterpart, plainly questions whether marriage even involved choice or freedom of movement for women: "Moralists are as much inclined to prescribe rules for the choice of a husband, as of a friend. I am afraid that the very title they prefix to their admonitions is apt to mislead a young mind" (101). In West's view, then, women are decidedly cut off from the decision-making process in marrying. Without a net of sisterhood to rely upon, women are forced into alliances against their will. Foster prefers to paint an Edenic universe in which husbands conveniently die or live abroad, as in the case of Elvira. Female solitude is often a prescription for happiness in Foster's schema.

Julia Greenfield opts for a retreat from "the noise and bustle of the world," a place where we can "commune with our own hearts" (H. Foster 139). This letter, in which Julia Greenfield stresses retreat, sisterhood, and the values of education is in keeping with the themes of the novel. Outside of the boundaries of social discourse ("giddy amusements"), Julia experiences a sort of connubial bliss as she tastes the solicitude of the scholar: "Give me a mind to range the sylvan scene, and taste the blessings of the vernal day" (139). A preoccupation, then, with education replaces the preoccupation one would expect that these women would share about marriage. It seems as if incidences of marriage have been silenced by Foster, in favor of an alternate discourse of desire for education and filial affection.

Marriage is sometimes viewed as suspect territory in the course of the novel, especially in one letter of Harriot Henly. Having returned from a wedding, Harriot speaks plainly of her distaste for the occasion, and portrays its ghastly, doomed, false spectatorship. "I imagine such exhilarating scenes [are] designed to dispel the anxiety and thoughtfulness," she says of the participants, adding that if she were to wed, "I should choose to retire from the observation of those indifferent and unfeeling spectators" (134). Henly implores Cleora to "look around the world and see the great many unhappy marriages" (134). Married couples, in Harriot's view, even those "contracted with the brightest prospects," end up in states of "wretchedness for life" (134).

Harriot views courtship with equal suspicion. "So many are the deceptions which love and courtship impose upon their votaries," she deliberates, "that I believe it difficult for the parties to judge impartially, or to discern the faults, where they only look for virtues" (135). Harriot ends her philippic against marriage and courtship by inviting Cleora to Boston. Harriot's effusive display of filial affection, combined with her characterization of their friendship, and juxtaposed with the preceding display of distaste for marriage creates an atmosphere of romantic friendship between women: "When do you come to Boston, Cleora? I am impatient for your society; because your friendship is void of flattery, and your sincerity and cheerfulness are always agreeable and advantageous. Adieu. HARRIOT HENLY" (135). Harriot Henly's letter in the context of Cleora's response, may be read as an early exemplification of the open discussion about lesbian love. Lillian Faderman reminds us that critics have suppressed lesbianism because they have regarded it "primarily as a sexual act and were unwilling to give it the dimensions they might attribute to a serious male-female love relationship" (37).

Cleora Partridge's response to Harriot Henly clearly jests about the possibility of a romantic friendship between these women. Cleora takes a distinctively humorous, even cynical tone with her friend. "Indeed, Harriot," she writes, "I open your letters with as much gravity as I would a sermon; you have such a knack for moralizing upon every event!" (H. Foster 136). Cleora agrees with Harriot in her opinions about marriage, yet she firmly resolves herself to such a union. "I must acknowledge it a weighty affair; and what you say has, perhaps, too much truth in it to be jested with" (136), she writes after disinviting Harriot from her wedding: "Your presence, I fear, would put such a restraint upon me, as to render me quite foolish and awkward in my appearance" (136). Cleora's allusion to the "awkward" feeling Harriot apparently gives her bespeaks a possible former lesbian union, which is further supported by her flippant suggestion of a "Boston marriage": "I believe, therefore, we had better resolve not to risk the consequences of a wrong choice, or imprudent conduct; but wisely devote ourselves to celibacy. I am sure we should make a couple of very clever old maids. If you agree to this proposition, we will begin in season to accustom ourselves to the virtues and habits of a single life" (136).

Cleora then pokes fun at Harriot's feminism. She reasons, "In this way we shall be useful to many of our own sex" (136). Cleora invites Harriot to live with her in union. "I wish to become a general reformer," she tells Harriot, adding flirtatiously, "If you approve it, dismiss your long train of admirers immediately and act not the part of a coquette[;] . . . we must rise above such narrow views, and let the world know that we act from principle" (137). These comments, while made in jest, bespeak the overriding concerns of the author and allow for a site of discussion of female love and female political thought. Even if Cleora Partridge dismisses Harriot Henly's love for her and professes her desire to participate in patriarchal society, her letter stands as a textual evidence of the existence of unspoken desires among women, both lesbian love and political opinions.

It is Cleora's rebuff that displays the characteristics of Harriot's desire, but it is her final dismissal, along with her admission of a feeling of "awkwardness" in Harriot's presence, that ultimately speaks of a possible past lesbian union. Cleora closes her letter: "by renouncing a connection which must be doubtful as to the issue" (137). Cleora fears societal remonstrations against lesbian love. She fears that their connection "will certainly expose me to the mortification of being looked at, when [she] is married" (173). "Farewell" says Cleora to Harriot, with a final dismissal of their prior friendship. By mouthing homophobia and anti-feminist remarks through Cleora Partridge, Hannah Webster Foster weaves the voice of the dominant ideology into her patchwork narrative. The use of humor allows for the discussion of subjects Foster obviously wishes to address—celibacy, feminism, lesbianism, and heterosexual marriage. In this case, Foster uses dialogism to voice opinions through another's voice.

It would be reductionist to read the letter as Foster's embrace of the dominant ideology spoken by one of her players. Instead, we should note that Foster masterfully constructs a double-edged tongue for Cleora Partridge. On the one hand, Cleora Partridge is emblematic of narrow-minded patriarchal society, but on the other hand, she mouths Foster's views, even if deriding them. One paragraph, in particular, stands out as an example of this technique. In discussing their proposed celibate union, Cleora suddenly adopts a completely serious tongue in defense of spinsterhood: "The world needs such examples as we might become; and if we can be instrumental of retrieving old-maidism from the imputation of ill-natured, oddity, and many other mortifying charges, which are now brought against it, I believe we shall save many a good girl from an unequal and unhappy marriage. It might have a salutary effect on the other sex too" (137). Foster's use of a double-edged tongue in Cleora Partridge allows for the author to write herself into the material and to infuse an argument for celibacy and commentary against heterosexual union into the discourse of the novel. Foster chooses to have a homophobic character speak her mind, subverting the confines of regulated discourse. Additionally, Foster manifests homophobia in the context of the discourse among women.

Clearly, these choices articulate the unsuppressed desire for a dialogue about female sexuality and its constraints in patriarchal culture. Other incidences of seemingly lesbian sexual love step out of the patchwork narrative of *The Boarding School*. Sophia Manchester's letter to Laura Guilford is a sensuous love letter of filial affection presaging the sisterly love of Laura and Lizzie in Christina Rossetti's poem "Goblin Market." Sophia offers Laura a "nosegay," a poem of "remembrance" in which Sophia seemingly oversteps the boundaries of "cordial" love:

From Laura's lips with wit replete.
The myrtle with the laurel bound,

And purple amaranths crown'd,
Within this little knot unite,
Like Laura's charms, to give delight.

(141)

As Carroll Smith-Rosenberg reminds us, Bakhtin stated that female novelists use diverse voices for the "covert expression of contradictions and
conflicts inherent in the ideologies and discourses of the times" (167).
The cacophony of voices in *The Boarding School* represent a heteroge-
neous mix of female dialogisms. Smith-Rosenberg's comment that "power
runs through this cacophony" (163) could not be more applicable than
to the case of Sophia Manchester's love letter to Laura Guilford. The voice
of lesbian sexuality acquires power through unsilencing same sex sexuality, which was considered nonexistent, if not a dangerous subversion
of early American patriarchy.

Foster's narrators predate those found by Joanne Dobson in nineteenth-
century women's novels, by "Saying 'yes' to society's expectations [while]
they also say 'No'—not in thunder or in lightning, but in small electric
whispers that run insistently through their conforming narratives" (240).
Foster foregrounds women who claim power over their bodies, who use
constructs of virtue to create and articulate the need for public female
selves. In this manner, Foster subverts male paradigms of virtue, which
have so often been used historically to oppress women. By connecting
the act of writing with the tenets of virtue, Foster inadvertently teaches,
through the character of the preceptress and through the polyvocal
tongues of the letter-writing pupils, that writing is virtuous, that women
must write the body.

Like *The Coquette*, which Kristie Hamilton sees as a skillful rhetorical locale in which "the disparity between codes of behavior in [the] two
spheres is made problematic" (135), *The Boarding School* poses questions through its use of a polyvocal narrative. A case in point is a letter
from T. Selby to the Reverend Boyer, ostensibly an exchange between male
friends about the "coquette" Miss Eliza Wharton, whom the Reverend
plans to marry. While some of the letter consists of information about
the character of Miss Wharton, Foster interrupts the male dialogue and
uses T. Selby to mouth her political ideology. In the midst of a description of Miss Wharton's charms, T. Selby recounts a party in which evolved
a free discussion of women's interest in politics. Miss Wharton and Mrs.
Richman agree that women ought to have the rights and privileges of the
patriotic male. They seek the label *patriot*, which had been denied women
in early America: "If the community flourish and enjoy health and freedom, shall we not share in the happy effects? If it be oppressed and disturbed, shall we not endure our proportion of evil? Why then should the
love of our country be a masculine passion only?" (44).

The women in Foster's work seek the solicitudes of freedom not only in a political context but in sexual politics as well. Eliza Wharton, the coquette who is tragically "undone" by the end of the novel, will be remembered for her voicing from the margins of society a desire for freedom in her choice of sexual partners: "What a pity, my dear Lucy, that the graces and virtues are not oftener united! They must, however, meet in the man of my choice; and till I find such a one, I shall continue to subscribe my name Eliza Wharton" (22). Some critics feel that Foster's *Coquette* never seriously challenges the power of the patriarchy. This is true in part, if one receives the book in the context of male literary technique. But if one reads *The Coquette* as a covert attack on marriage and courtship, one can begin to see Foster as an early feminist who wished to expose the lack of freedom women had over their bodies in early America, especially within the confines of courtship and marriage behavior. In both *The Boarding School* and *The Coquette*, it is women who freely and casually have sexual relations with men who suffer the most harsh consequences in society. In *The Coquette*, Eliza Wharton dies in childbirth, alone and ostracized at a boarding house. Foster paints similarly grim endings in *The Boarding School* for women who attempt to have sexual freedom. These portrayals come in the form of the allegories that the preceptress includes in her valedictory address.

It is important to note that Foster chooses to incorporate the allegories of seduced and abandoned bad girls with the dominating narrative of the preceptress's parental role, rather than include them in the epistles of the female pupils of the boarding school. In this manner, Foster allows for the epistolary section to represent a site in which female discourse is uninterruptable, safe, and a site of the female coming of age. The valedictory address, then, is monologic, more in keeping with traditional male-defined Aristotelian discourse. The voice of the preceptress is parental, unmutable: domineering and admonishing, yet soothing and encouraging. The allegories are completely hyperbolic, and the preceptress acts as a preacher might, constructing polar opposites of good and evil and admonishing the listening pupils to "view them now" (13).

Each allegorical figure has an opposite in didactic address of the preceptress. Belinda, who is ruined by idleness, is contrasted with Clara, a widow who sells her needlework to survive (10–13). But idleness is far the lesser of evils in Foster's hierarchy. Juliana represents the coquette who willingly rushes into sexual union with a "coxcomb" (20). Juliana is met with a fate not unlike that of the coquette, but here Foster deals up a twist of psychological horror upon her character. Juliana is tortured by the guilt of her father's death, whose "sorrow and vexation preyed so deeply [that he] . . . dies without again facing his undutiful and ruined daughter" (22). Juliana is further undone by her husband, who spends her inheritance and the joins his regiment and leaves her in "poverty and neglect" (22). Eliza

Wharton may have escaped the brutal punishment Foster hands out to Juliana, who is left in her "emaciated form, her squalid appearance" completely friendless and destitute. In Foster's handling, the death of Eliza Wharton seems far less cruel than the loss of sisterhood Juliana experiences: "the kindness and love of her best friends!" (23). The female body, in Foster's texts, is often the site of punishment and surveillance.

Flirtilla, a beautiful coquette, is punished in the narrative with a case of smallpox: "View her now, peevish, discontented and gloomy!" (54). Levitia, an actress who elopes and ends up a "courtezan," causing the death of her mother and the ill health of her father, is nearly killed by a fever, "which ruined her beauty, ruined her voice, and left her without a means of support" (49). Needless to say, Levitia's lover abandons her, and she is finally "despised and avoided by all her former acquaintance, and must inevitably spend the remainder of her days in wretchedness" (49). Amelia, who did not take religion seriously, is "attacked by a violent cold" (108) and subsequently becomes a sign of the gravity of religious obligation: "That even the youth are not exempt from the arrest of [the] universal conqueror, the tombstone of Amelia will tell you" (108). The allegorical figures of "good" female behavior in the valedictory address of the preceptress are not so much women who marry well as women who manage well on their own and who exhibit charity to their female compatriots. This is more in keeping with the ideological framework of sisterhood found in the epistolary letters of the pupils. Matilda, for example, is praised for teaching her maid how to mend. This instance happens to cross barriers of class as well as support the ideology of sisterhood. Matilda stresses the usefulness of weaving as a source of revenue for economic empowerment: "By this means you may learn a very useful lesson, I assure you, a lesson, which by practicing for yourself, will enable you to lay up part of your wages against the time when sickness or old age shall take you from your labors" (14).

As an allegorical figure, Lucinda empowers herself financially by taking over the family business. Foster will use any means of hyperbolic narrative to infuse her ideological concerns into the address of the Preceptress. Here, for example, Lucinda gets an opportunity to show her competence in the public sphere only after a highly overwrought story in which her mother dies and her father goes (temporarily) insane: "[S]he could not reconcile herself to the idea of her father's depending on charity for subsistence. Yet what could be done? One resource only remained;—her own exertions" (38). Foster carefully weaves specific instructions on how to reclaim the family business for her female audience: "She therefore devoted herself to the business without delay; examined her father's accounts, collected whatever remained that was valuable; sold the superfluous moveables, and purchased a small stock for trade" (38). In a narrative move calculated to support the dominant patriarchy, though, Foster writes Lucinda's father back into sanity, and he reclaims the business, "and live[s] to see his children all well provided for, and happily settled around him" (38). In this particular allegory, Foster fails to complete the model of a competent free woman who can survive both the public and private worlds, but nevertheless the instructive matter at the heart of the Lucinda narrative bespeaks Foster's wish that her female readership will use her advice and become financially independent in their own right.

As Judith Lowder Newton notes, "Women's writing may be both the locus of compensating fantasies and the site of protest, actions expressive of the author's power" (11). Hannah Webster Foster's *Boarding School* exhibits a female author expressing her power through the voice of the Preceptress and through the polyvocal metonymy of the epistolary letters. Linda Kerber recognizes Hannah Webster Foster as one of the "central architects of the new female ideology" of what would develop into "Republican Motherhood" (11). Women such as Hannah Webster Foster, Susannah Rowson, and Phillis Wheatley were, in the period in which they held limited dominance over the forms of textual production available to women, recontextualizing concepts of virtue and the female body. Their voices of sisterly or motherly advice and concern constitute evidence of early women writers' insistence on a need to create a public female self in a society dedicated to suppressing the female body (while ironically also dedicated to freedom of the "individual"). This is not to suggest that Foster or these other early American women writers were writing out of any sort of planned "integrity or totality" as a tool against the dominant ideology of the day. Instead, women subverted and supported the dominant ideology at their choosing.

The Boarding School reveals Hannah Webster Foster's attempt to write the female body, in both a subversive and nonsubversive manner. Foster herself attended a boarding school, so perhaps we can surmise that she was writing from her own experience on some level. (Apparently, she taught her children some of the same female-empowering virtues that the Preceptress teaches her pupils. Two of her daughters, Eliza Lanesford Cushing and Harriet Vaughan Cheney, became writers.) *The Boarding School* is a finely woven narrative that makes proficient use of the fluid "patchwork" or "polyvocal" narrative described (in Bakhtin's terms) as a style that reflected a political resistance at the margins of dominant forms of societal discourse.

The Boarding School at times seems to adhere to male standards of propriety, as seen mainly in the opening valedictory address of the Preceptress. However, the epistolary letters speak of an artfully subversive early woman writer fragmenting patriarchal ideology. Foster's *Coquette* shares an equally fervent, if more covert, attempt to question the dominant ideology. *The Boarding School* takes Foster's agenda a step further. It presents a community of female voices articulating suppressed desires for female education, sisterhood, same sex union, celibacy, financial independence, and perhaps what is most important, the desire for political equality and the reclaimed female body.

5

Early African American Instruction and Correction: The Case of Frances E. W. Harper

The newly recovered novel *Minnie's Sacrifice* (1869), written by renowned African American author Frances E. W. Harper and originally published as a serial publication in the *Christian Recorder*, is an excellent early exemplification of African American conduct literature. As Frances Smith Foster writes in her introduction to *Minnie's Sacrifice*, it is important that we "focus upon the fact that *Minnie's Sacrifice* was published in a black paper, by a black woman, for black readers—during Reconstruction (xxix–xxx). It is also important to keep in mind the fact that Frances E. W. Harper, like many other early African American authors, appropriates and renarrates Judeo-Christian mythology as African American political literature in this novel, as she does in her poetry and other novels. In fact, Foster sees this novel as "a deliberate retelling of the Old Moses story" (xxx). Briefly, the novel concerns two main African American characters, Minnie and Louis, who, in unrelated (but parallel) narratives are sent to the North to be educated and to pass as white. Both are the children of a white master and a black female slave, though both are brought up to believe they are white. Minnie grows up to be fiercely antislavery, and Louis grows up to be proslavery and to fight as a soldier for the rebel Confederates. The sentimental novel provides a terrific scaffold on which to build the events of irony and subversive wit. In a characteristic trope of the sentimental novel, both characters eventually learn of their parentage and have to decide if they are willing to "pass" as "white," and, predictably, they fall in love.

However, much is unpredictable in *Minnie's Sacrifice*. It is a fascinating example of cultural appropriation and renarration of tales and tale-telling styles that are used to instruct. The Christian theme of the novel should in no way be determined as a one-way cultural appropriation. I do not wish to suggest this idea. Instead, I wish to take into account Frances Smith Foster's reminder: "If we were to take seriously the idea that Christianity was not manufactured in Europe and did in fact contain beliefs and practices common to many African religions and the idea that in many African cultures, poetry was used to instruct, correct, and commemorate, then Phillis Wheatley might be read as an audacious, even a subversive, poet" (xxiv). I wish to extend Foster's thesis to apply it to Frances E. W. Harper's novel, *Minnie's Sacrifice*, a novel that is indeed politically subversive yet categorically Christian African American. Therefore, when I use the terms *appropriate* and *renarrate,* I do not refer to the Christian tropes and tales themselves, but to the fascinating manner in which Harper constructs a tale that allows her to place the language of the African American in the months of "white" characters and vice versa. Further complicating matters, Harper, at times, blurs the distinction between "black" and "white," thus undermining the categories themselves and exposing them as distinctly specious constructions.

Harper freely appropriates the voice and tone of the African American preacher as well. Indeed, there seems to be little distinction between the style of the pulpit and the style of speech and writing in much early African American writing. Though it is delightful to read, as Foster reminds us, "Francis Harper's writings were functional and theological" (xxvii). It is as didactic as it is sentimental.

I would like to consider an early passage in *Minnie's Sacrifice* that marks Harper's ability to appropriate the tongue of a white character, Camilla, and places in her mouth a choice biblical narrative for political purposes. Camilla will later save the young Louis who is born blonde and fair and whose mother has died. First, however, Harper sets her up as a figure reminiscent of the Old Testament Moses story. The author calls upon the use of the improbable and appropriates and renarrates it to suit her purpose. Camilla muses out loud, in chapter 1, that she wonders if she could save young Louis from being a slave: "I was reading yesterday a beautiful story in the Bible about a wicked king, who wanted to kill all the little boys of a people who were enslaved in his land, and how his mother hid her child by the side of the river, and that the king's daughter found him and saved his life. It was a fine story; and I read it till I cried. Now I mean to do something like that good princess" (5). One of the great pleasures of reading this novel is noting the author's clever use of improbable situations and events and equally improbable pronouncements, especially from the mouths of the white characters in the novel. Frequently, Harper appropriates whiteness and renarrates it to suit her political purposes. She spends far more time characterizing and representing white people in *Minnie's Sacrifice* than she does African American people. In fact, Harper avoids stereotyping whites by recreating them in the process of appropriation and renarration.

Pain and anguish come through strongly in Frances Harper's poetry, especially in "A Double Standard" and "An Appeal to My Country-women," and it is translated and inculcated into political action through language in such poems as "She's Free," "The Crocuses," and "Learning to Read." But the fascinating way in which Harper refashions whiteness in *Minnie's Sacrifice*, a sentimental novel that moves beyond stereotype and transforms pain into political literary action, includes Harper's creation of white characters in black skin. The tongue-seizing she engages in is utterly remarkable and sometimes almost postmodern in its implications. Harper often puts African American tales in white characters' mouths to further her political agenda and also to heighten her storytelling with wit and irony. In chapter 2, for example, Camilla again disrupts the white plantocratic landscape with antislavery rhetoric, this time literally renarrating a story told by a family slave, Isaac. After returning from an abolitionist meeting, Camilla's father refutes everything he has just heard at the meeting. He asks Camilla if she believed what she heard, and she responds: "Why yes, Pa, I did, because our Isaac used to tell me just such a story as that. If I had shut my eyes, I could have imagined that it was Isaac telling the story" (13). Camilla then proceeds to recount a long story told to her by Isaac about how he lost his wife to a slave trader. Camilla is an extraordinary white representation. She has a thoroughly decolonized mind. Harper creates a white character that is made of "sympathy and compassion" and a "sense of justice" (15). She is not patronizing toward African Americans, however. Harper carefully explains how it came to be that Camilla understands the position of African American slaves. Even in the preposterous unreal world of the sentimental novel, Harper recognizes the need to give her characters realistic motivations: "She had lived so much among the slaves, and had heard so many tales of sorrow breathed confidentially in her ears, that she had unconsciously imbibed their view of the matter; and without comprehending the injustice of the system, she had learned to view it from their standpoint of observation" (15).

Camilla continually argues with her father, Le Croix. Essentially, their arguments boil down to the standard abolition debates. Le Croix invokes the typical, tired antiabolitionist rhetoric, for example, that "the Negroes are contented" (14) under slavery. Camilla refutes the points not with abolitionist rhetoric, but by recounting real experiences of African Americans (known secondhand to her). This brilliant novelistic device thus offers the reader an abolitionist debate mouthed by white people who are penned by an African American woman. As a game, the debate is like a loaded deck. Camilla is free to "backtalk" her father because the novelist allows it; and she is a better abolitionist speaker because she is voicing the opinions and tales of African American slaves themselves, rather than using Northern abolitionist rhetoric. This is an important point because it suggests that Harper is catering to her black readership by using the white character as a mouthpiece. The section is charged with deeply subversive political humor that would seem to privilege the black readership by offering a unique situation that could perhaps only take place in the confines of this sentimental novel.

Camilla's use of what Bakhtin dubbed "internally persuasive discourse" (*Dialogic* 342), is a challenge to authoritative discourse of white supremacy. As a mouthpiece, Camilla is speaking in an African American tongue; she is telling the story of the African American slave using a form of internally persuasive discourse, or as it is defined by Bakhtin, "retelling a text in one's own words, with one's own accents, gestures, modifications" (424). Harper uses internally persuasive discourse throughout the novel, and she uses it in different ways, invoking a myriad of heteroglossia (speaking another's tongue) from "white" characters telling African American tales to "black" characters telling "white" tales. Harper's novel exposes the oppositional politics of the African American sentimental novel, proving the thesis of Bakhtin, who wrote that the sentimental novel "opposes the quasi-elevated and false heteroglossia found in literary language, which is subject to exposure and invalidation by sentimentalism and its discourse" (397).

Nowhere is this challenge more apparent than in the almost postmodern self-reflective section in which Minnie, a young African American who has been brought up to believe she is white, recounts a story she heard about a young "white" girl who was sent home from school because it was discovered that the young woman was "part" African American. Minnie tells this story-within-a-story, a palimpsest of her own story, to her adoptive parents, Anna and Thomas, who agonize over whether or not they should tell Minnie that she herself is "part" African American. The incident is prefaced by a long speech, typical of Minnie, who of course, thinking she is white, employs dialogized (double-voiced) discourse. However, her words challenge the authoritative white supremacist discourse around her. Here, Harper retells African American tales in an African American tongue, in an unusual form, some might say a "hybrid" form of internally persuasive discourse, unusual in that Minnie is speaking for her "own people" even though she is not aware of it. This discourse is politically charged and calls attention to its creator because of its self-reflectivity. It announces itself as a construct and playfully engages the reader in a way not unlike the talking book. It signifies as it exposes and disturbs the hegemonic order of white privilege and replaces it with black authorial privilege. At the same time it "works" within the confines of the sentimental novel, it is playful, absurd, yet politically charged and perfectly plausible in this genre. It must have been intensely meaningful for a black contemporary reader to hear Minnie tell her white foster mother, "I do think it must be dreadful to be a colored person in this country; how I should suffer if I knew that I was hated and despised for what I couldn't help. Oh, it must be dreadful to be colored" (46).

The passage is laden with humor but also fear of that which is hidden. Harper draws this out to considerable lengths, putting the white foster mother, Anna, in the uncomfortable position of having to hear her African American foster daughter come uncomfortably close to figuring out her own story, while enumerating the evils of white American supremacy. For the most part, Anna stands silently listening, a white woman listening to an African American daughter. In response to Minnie's last remark, Anna meekly suggests that "God never makes any mistakes" (46), lest Minnie begin to wonder about her own lineage. As Anna waits and listens to one of Minnie's many tirades against the poor treatment of African Americans, the author takes the liberty of the sentimental novel to infuse a speaking African American character with authoritative discourse as she silences the white listener. This has a performative element that should not go unrecognized. It places the white reader in a position of listening and a black reader in a position of directly engaging in the performative in an identification position with the language of the African American woman, who, again, it must be noted, mistakenly assumes she is white. Their conversation is one-sided and unusual. Minnie preaches to her foster mother at length: "[B]ut, mother, it must be hard to be forced to ride in smoking cars; to be insulted in the different thoroughfares of travel; to be denied access to public resorts in some places,—such as lecture halls, theatres, concerts, and even have a particular seat assigned in churches, and sometimes feel you were even an object of pity to your best friends" (46). Any audience, regardless of color, would find, I think, considerable interest in this passage because of the reasons listed above, because of the heightened risk of unveiling, and because the passage hints strongly at the future of Minnie, who is bound (by convention) to be "found out" and bound to experience some of the very scorn and rejection she describes in her own speech.

The above event is matched with a parallel event in the life of Louis, who has been raised to think he is white and has adopted racist and antiabolitionist attitudes. Harper describes the complexity of Louis's relationship with the South. She stresses the importance of the fact that Louis was educated in the North but feels compelled to defend the South as if the South were his mother. Ironically, of course, his real mother, unbeknownst to him, was an African American slave. "He is strongly Southern in his feelings, but having been educated in the North . . . he feels a sense of honor in defending the South. She is his mother, he says, and that man is an ingrate who will not stand by his mother and defend her when she is in peril" (36).

In a fit of patriotic fervor, Louis later announces his plan to immediately become a Confederate soldier. He gets in an argument with his sister, Camilla, "a strong union woman," and the subject escalates to the point where his real grandmother, Miriam, reveals his African American parentage: "[Y]ou, Louis Le Croix, white as you look, are colored, and you are my own daughter's child, and if it had not been for Miss Camilla, who's been such an angel to you, you would have been a slave to-day, and then you wouldn't have been a confederate" (59). It is interesting to note that Harper heightens the impact of the African American woman speaker, who leaves Louis "as pale as death, trembling like a leaf." Minnie's real mother, who reveals Minnie's "secret," is equally powerful: "Minnie trembled from head to foot; a deadly pallor overspread her cheek, and she stood still as if rooted to the ground in silent amazement" (50). Harper later returns the topic to motherhood, again pointing out the irony of Louis's earlier comments, by putting these words in Louis's mouth: "I can never raise my hand against my mother's race" (60).

Louis's language, whether it is uttered when he is aware he is African American or when he falsely believes he is white, is dialogized. It is charged with double-voicedness. When he is an African American speaking in a white tongue, his speech is dialogic, as is Minnie's when she speaks in a white body. The fluidity designed by Harper that allows these characters to move among and between black and white speech points out the level of constructedness of American conceptions of race and allows for slippage between the categories of "white" and "black." Indeed, Harper's embrace of heteroglossia, her construction of characters who speak in another's tongue, deconstructs race and exposes it as primarily a social construct. This is one of the conceits of novels and narratives of passing, and it brings up, inevitably, the difficulties of definition wrought upon people of "mixed race" or people who are "part" African American and "part" white. I emphasize my quotation marks around these terms, as I do not wish to embrace them. Nor did Harper. Harper questions the notion of a construct routinely accepted as "whiteness." She goes to great pains to explain the ethnic background of Louis's and Minnie's "white" side. Both are descendants of a Spanish grandmother and a French grandfather who immigrated from Haiti. Harper equally questions the "one drop rule" applied to anyone who had any African American blood.

Both Louis and Minnie, having lived in the socially constructed world of whiteness, are in some ways privileged by their passing experience. They speak from a point of view that is itself dialogized and double-voiced. When asked why she does not simply continue to pass for white, Minnie explains her reasoning: "[T]o tell you the truth, having passed most of my life in white society, I did not feel that the advantages of that society would have ever paid me for the loss of my self-respect, by passing as white, when I knew that I was colored; when I knew that any society, however cultivated, wealthy or refined, would not be a social gain to me, if my color and not my character must be my passport of admission" (72). Minnie's words are charged by the dialogism of speaking both in a "white" tongue and a "black" tongue. She cannot be reduced to a biological essence. Her words challenge a "white" supremacist society in a manner that is unusual because of her ability to see from both "sides," and she cuts to the falsity of this artificial construction. However, it must be remembered that Minnie is a product of the imagination of the African American writer herself.

Harper constructs Minnie and Louis as characters who freely appropriate and renarrate whiteness in order to critique it as a category and to critique white society in double-voiced characters that attack American systemic apartheid from a white perspective, a black perspective, and even a male and female perspective. It is a stunning use of the sentimental novel genre, and it is as much an astonishing literary achievement as it is a political achievement.

If Harper is remarkably adept at treating black characters who critique whiteness (in both a "white" and "black" tongue), she is equally adept at creating white characters who also critique white politics and hegemony. For example, Josiah Collins, a white character who helps to place the child Minnie in the hands of some Northern Quaker friends, is particularly outspoken about racism among the Northern abolitionists. He is cautious because, as he states, "There are a number of our people in the North, who do two things. They hate slavery and hate Negroes" (20).

Later in the novel, Josiah and Anna both debate Northern and Southern white attitudes toward African Americans. In chapter 6, this debate occurs, and Harper uses the white speakers as black rhetoricians in a form of heteroglossia (speaking an/other's tongue) that amounts to what might be characterized as "white minstrelsy." It is a fairly lengthy passage that is rife with African American humor, understanding, and rhetoric. It seems highly unusual for these two white characters to debate such a topic at length. Indeed, I cannot help but conclude that Harper is herself speaking with tongue in cheek through these white characters. In a dialogic that fuses humor with serious political questions, Josiah and Anna perform a white-faced minstrelsy that gestures to the black audience as if to wink and encourage their participation in the debate.

At the beginning of the chapter, Josiah has just arrived in the North, traveling via the Underground Railroad and seeking to place Minnie with Quaker abolitionist foster parents. He invites the audience in on the (bitter) humor he finds in "passing" the girl off as white: "I was really amused with the attention she received from the Southern ladies; knowing how they would have shrunk from such offices if they had known that one drop of the outcast blood ran in her veins" (27). The political relevance of such a remark, placed in the mouth of a white speaker, is truly important. With this use of the "inside joke," the humor is itself a form of conduct literature, a witty and complex form of social critique that is just one example of Harper's shrewd ability to assume the role of social arbiter. The comment not only lambastes the "one drop rule," but it also harshly criticizes the racist behavior of Southern women. Immediately afterward, Anna responds by beginning the discussion on prejudice in the North and South. Anna states: "Why Josiah, I have always heard that there was more prejudice against the colored people in the North than in the South. . . . We see in many parts of the North a very few of the colored people, and our impressions of them have received their coloring more or less from what the slaveholders have said of them" (28).

One cannot help but think of Anna as a performer in whiteface, a figure of Harper's imagination, and it is indeed highly charged humor to place these words in the mouth of a "white" speaker, a Northerner criticizing white Northern behavior. The reader is inclined to roll one's eyes toward heaven over the next series of remarks in which Anna mouths the common platitudes that must have been prevalent, platitudes that supposedly "excuse" Northern white racism on the basis that it is only learned from the South. Anna continues: "We have been taught that they [African Americans] are idle, improvident, and unfitted for freedom, and incapable of progression" (27–28). However, Anna adds that the main difference she sees between Northern and Southern attitudes toward blacks is that Southerners seem to have less "horror of personal contact" (28) with blacks. This statement is a jaw-dropper because it is an admission, from the mouth of a Northern white woman, that Northerners indeed are deeply racist and that they have a fear of personal contact with the same people they profess to love and wish to unshackle from the bounds of slavery. One cannot help but think of the speaker as an African American creation, speaking in whiteface, criticizing her own behavior, as well as that of her own race, religion, and region. But the criticism is not simply of Northern whites. Josiah responds with a long invective against Southern prejudice. He says that "it is a prejudice against their rising in the scale of humanity. A prejudice which virtually says you are down, and I mean to keep you down. As a servant I tolerate you; you are as useful as you are valuable, but rise one step in the scale of being, and I am ready to put you down" (28). Josiah's speech, if we think of it as a form of whiteface minstrelsy, punctuates the sentimental novel with politically subversive intent. Josiah spends considerable time listing the offensive and racist character of the white Southerners, who treat free blacks as "the outcasts of an outcast race" (28) and deny them free association, free assembly, and the right to give public testimony; "in the case of outrages, [they are] denied their [right] of testimony" (28). This last point is an important one, as it self-reflexively applies to this speech (and the text of the novel) itself. It calls our attention to the issue of African American testimony and tale telling. It makes us doubly aware that we are reading the words of an African American female speaker who is testifying and signifying through her white players who perform on-stage, essentially in a black venue, in whiteface and in dialogized speech that is charged with meaning. Harper is not only exercising her right to public testimony, but she is calling to attention the many cases of outrage that are perpetrated against the African American peoples, both in the North and in the South. By appropriating white bodies as speakers, puppets of the author, Harper demonstrates brilliant technical and rhetorical flair. She not only sets up a debate in which African Americans get to testify, but she sets up the debate so that the whites themselves both agree to their prejudice and testify to it publicly.

After Josiah's harsh critique of the South, Anna uses her tongue against Northerners, specifically Philadelphians: "But, Josiah, we have much to blush for in Pennsylvania; colored people are denied the privilege of riding on our streetcars. Only last week when I was in Philadelphia, I saw a very decent-looking colored woman with a child, who looked too feeble to walk, and the child too heavy for her to carry. She beckoned to a conductor, but he swept by and took no more heed of her than if she had been a dog" (28–29). After this story, the debate veers off into a Quaker friend's meeting. Anna's husband, Thomas, joins the discussion, and the debate turns to the question of how to solve racism. Again, Josiah is Harper's mouthpiece, emphasizing that in order for there to be racial equality, the African American must acquire land. The discussion veers toward a comparison of African Americans with Jews, in what seems to be a critique of whites' continual comparison between the plight of the Jewish people and the slaves. While both agree that the Jews have a lengthy ancestry, Josiah comments that he does not think "the Negro can trace with certainty his origin back to any of the older civilizations" (30) and that this impedes the ability of his race to move forward toward equality. Here Harper attacks the problematic notion popularized in white America that African Americans have no cultural background in any older civilizations. While the author does not go to great lengths to deny this problematic but pervasive attitude, she does often make the reader question the notion of "civilization" and "civil" behavior in white America. For example, Georgette, the epitome of Southern white womanhood, is harshly criticized when she sells off Minnie for a set of pearls. This incident comes at the beginning of the novel, when a Northern woman mistakes Minnie for a daughter of Georgette. Georgette responds by brutally cutting Minnie's hair off and insisting that she be sold. Her husband pretends to sell the child and offers Georgette pearls as a peace offering. Here, the author interjects, in her own voice: "What mattered it to her if every jewel cost a heart throb, and if the whole set were bought with the price of blood? They suited her style of beauty, and she cared not what they lost.

Proud, imperious, and selfish, she knew no law but her own will; no gratification but the enjoyment of her own desires" (21). The "civilization" of the South is called into question here. Harper pulls no punches in her invective against Southern white women in such passages. She is equally powerful in her indictment against Southern white men. For example, she compares white Southerners who take sexual advantage of slaves to Satan himself. Ellen, the dead mother of Minnie, had been taken advantage of by Louis Le Grange, when he was "in just that mood of which it is said that Satan finds some mischief for idle hands to do" (23). Her mother, Milly, tried to protect Ellen but "saw her child engulfed, as thousands of her race had been" (23).

Minnie and Louis are charged with the task of inventing a new civilization. When both accept their race, they marry and begin a school for African Americans. Minnie becomes Harper's mouthpiece for political rhetoric of African American revolution: "She felt it was no mean nor common privilege to be the pioneer of a new civilization[;] . . . how much higher and holier must his or her work be who dispenses light, instead of darkness, knowledge, instead of ignorance, and over the ruins of the slave-pen and auction-block erects institutions of learning" (67–68). Minnie is an emblem of liberation theology. She will not be satisfied until there is "an army of civilizers; the army of the pen, and not the sword" (68). Minnie and Louis boldly assert their rights to testify and signify. They are unique as black rhetoricians and in some ways as characters because of their shared experience in passing for white. Their words are doubly dialogized. Their double-voicedness is mirrored by the fact that they are privileged to be able to speak from both white and black positions and life experience. They confound essentialism.

Because of the unusually large number of debates, *Minnie's Sacrifice* is perhaps unusually well crafted to present political questions to these African American characters. There is little they do not debate, from the future of the black race to vote bribing and women's suffrage. In one such discussion, Louis remarks that it is not yet time for women to have the right to vote. "This hour belongs to the Negro" (78), he says, giving Minnie ample opportunity to instruct the reader why women should have the right to vote: "But, Louis, is it not the Negro woman's hour also? . . . If you would have the government strong and enduring you should entrench it in the hearts of both the men and women of the land" (78–79).

Minnie convinces her husband and the reader. Minnie and Louis go on to do great work, and in a missing chapter, Minnie dies of unknown causes. Louis goes on to build a better society in the South, "until peace like bright dew . . . should reign triumphant where violence and slavery had held their carnival of shame and crime for ages" (90).

In the concluding chapter, Harper directly addresses the black reader. She is emphatic in her role of social and political leader: "We have wealth among us, but how much of it is ever spent in building the future of the race? In encouraging talent, and developing genius?" (91). Harper also criticizes black authors who created "tragic mulatto" characters: "While some authors of the present day have been writing their stories about white men marrying beautiful quadroon girls, who, in doing so were lost to us socially, I conceived of one of that same class to whom I gave a higher, holier destiny; a life of lofty self-sacrifice and beautiful self-consecration, finished at the post of duty, and rounded off with the fiery crown of martyrdom, a circlet which ever changes into a diadem of glory" (91). With polished rhetorical flourish, Harper emphasizes the importance of writing conduct literature in the form of the novel and the importance of creating positive African American women as role models and religious martyrs. In an appropriation of the rhetoric of the cult of true womanhood, Minnie is a model of self-sacrifice and self-consecration; she is an African American renarration of the cult of true womanhood as a political speaker, teacher, and martyr. She is remarkably like Harper herself, who appropriated and renarrated the construct of the cult of true womanhood to fit her own sense of self and her political agenda. Though she was a well-known orator, who began speaking for the Maine Anti-Slavery Society in 1854, Harper was described as "slender and graceful, with a soft musical voice" (F. Foster xiii). Frances Ellen Watkins Harper was one of the few women allowed to speak publicly at this time. She shared the dais with Frederick Douglass, Sojourner Truth, and other radical reform speakers. Her record of achievement as a politician is especially impressive given the fact that she was also a prolific author. She organized and served various professional and political organizations, from the National Council of Negro Women to the American Equal Rights Association. Societies were named in her honor, so well known was she as a speaker, leader, and journalist.

But Frances Ellen Watkins Harper is by no means the only early African American who could easily be considered a conduct writer. She is but one voice in a legion of black writers, such as Phillis Wheatley, Harriet Jacobs, Frederick Douglass, and Harriet E. Wilson, who wrote and spoke as social arbiters. Her legacy continues in the voices of Toni Morrison, bell hooks, Martin Luther King Jr., and Malcolm X, all of whom ultimately may be read as conduct writers in that their decolonized voices advocate changes in societal behavior.

6

Feasting on the Feminine: Emily Brontë's Poetic Discourse of Anticonduct

> So hopeless is the world without,
> The world within I doubly prize;
> Thy world where guile and hate and doubt
> And cold suspicion never rise;
> Where thou and I and Liberty
> Have undisputed sovereignty.
> What matters is that all around
> Danger and grief and darkness lie,
> If but within our bosom's bound
> We hold a bright unsullied sky,
> warm with ten thousand mingled rays
> Of suns that know no winter days?
> —Emily Brontë, "To Imagination"

Critics have long wrestled with the location and voice of Emily Brontë, who wrote under the pseudonym of Ellis Bell, hid her manuscripts, and disguised her selves within maddeningly complex, often renamed characters in the sagas of what has been collected as *Gondal's Queen*.

Indeed, it was the "world within" that Brontë "doubly prize[d]," and it is that world that I will attempt to demystify, at least to a small degree, through a textual examination of this poem. The work stands out as an exemplification of a Gothic empire Emily Brontë built for herself, within which she struggled to have "Liberty" and "undisputed sovereignty" over the external world of conduct that surveilled her every move. Emily Brontë demonstrated her need to control her universe not only through her writing but also through her willful denial of the pleasures of the body, particularly food and sleep. Brontë's anorexia, juxtaposed with her metaphoric feasting on the feminine, locates her desire to literally write her body.

A reading of Brontë's anorexic behavior as (in Albaraq Mahbobhah's words) a "defacement of a socially endorsed *prosopopeia* of male perfection" (91) suggests Brontë's rejection of a male *prosopopeia,* or mask, through her asceticism and simultaneous adoption of a female form of *prosopopeia*, in her writing. Brontë othered herself, masking her body and her poetry as a redefinition of the feminine. By marking her own body, she claimed herself as her own distinctive other. As Mahbobhah explains: "By trying to untangle herself from the web of the desires of her family members, the anorexic seeks to secure an Other, that is, to be independent" (89).

Julia Kristeva locates "food-loathing as perhaps the most elementary form of abjection," one in which "'I' become, 'I' give birth to myself" ("Adolescent" 3). Emily Brontë rejected the religious views of her father, the Reverend Patrick Brontë, particularly his articulation of patriarchal heaven. Brontë gives birth, then, to her own unorthodox construction of heaven, a female world of "stars" and night visitors associated with beauty and sexual desire. That she forced herself to hide her othered self in her dominant female poetic voices is proof of her cognizance of their subversive nature.

As Mahbobhah notes, the voice of the anorexic "is a defacement of patriarchal heaven" (93). Emily Brontë defaces her father's view of heaven and voices her desire for a female pantheistic vision, one in which she drinks (or feasts on) the gazes of feminine beings, in "Stars," for example. But even Brontë's feminine deities were forced to contend with the destructive gaze of the male deity. Brontë's introduction to an unforgiving male, omniscient presence was daily reinforced by her father's view of God, who reminds him of the "consciousness of his depravity and weakness, and a conviction that the best of his actions . . . could not stand the test of the All-Seeing Eye," as he wrote in *Cottage Poems* (19, 21). This "All-Seeing Eye" makes an appearance in "Stars." "His fierce beams" "strike" the brow of the narrator and invade Emily Brontë's version of heaven (226). "Stars" stands as a metaphor for a willful contest of the power structure in the Brontë household and, by extension, a contest of gender constructs in religion and society.

Emily Brontë, if not working from an active lesbian sexuality, is certainly adopting a flexible gendered image, one that "both deconstructs the heterosexual pattern of creativity and creates a space for redefining the relationship of the woman writer to other women writers, to readers, and to the text" (Farwell 101).

Marilyn R. Farwell's definition of a lesbian literary imagination allows for Emily Brontë's poetry to be seen as an arena in which the woman poet "affirms the need for women to rename ourselves," (103). Such a reading is in support of the reading of a "matriarchal mythology" located by Christine Gallant (80) in her study of the Gondal sagas. In "Stars" (1845), Emily Brontë performs repressed libidinous desires and locates the creative female in opposition to the restrictive codes of Victorian patriarchal society. Brontë's *prosopopeiac* other paradoxically invites one to read the suppressed female deities as hostages to patriarchally defined sunlight:

> O Stars and Dreams and Gentle Night;
> O Night and Stars return!
> And hide me from the hostile light
> That does not warm, but burn.
>
> (226)

The next stanza implicitly embraces lesbian sexuality as a spiritually redeeming force of feminine desire:

> That drains the blood of suffering men;
> Drinks tears, instead of dew:
> Let me sleep through his blinding reign,
> And only wake with you!
>
> (227)

The topos of a male sun as destroyer of female creation also can be found in other women poets, such as Emily Dickinson. Betsy Erkila suggests such a consistent use of imagery in Brontë and Dickinson in a comparison of the above passage with Dickinson's "The Sun—just touched the morning—" in which "a female dawn is left feeble and uncrowned by the blaze of the 'wheeling king.'" Erkila notes that "sealed off from the sun world, the dungeon becomes for both poets the locus and condition of female imaginative power" (64). "Stars" concludes with a plea for a fantasy world of sisterly love, a night world safe from the "blinding reign" of an oppressive patriarchy. Emily Brontë reclaims her sexuality and her body aesthetically in this poem, in which figures of the living dead battle for control of the female body in the privacy of the bedchamber.

Brontë's living dead female figure exerts self-control of the body after death, an impossible trope within Christian doctrine, but a prevalent and permissible one within female Gothicism and medieval mysticism. Brontë's fasting and visionary reclaiming of the body can be compared to that of the women mystics of the Middle Ages who practiced asceticism and renounced food for, as Carolyn Walker Bynum observes, "To repress eating and hunger was to control the body" (*Holy Feast* 2). Katherine Frank surmises that for Emily Brontë, "[w]riting and fasting are two available responses to conditions of helplessness and powerlessness. Both provide the illusion of mastery and control" (221). Emily denied food when she was feeling out of control, as when she was sent to Roe Head School. Nicknamed infamously "The General," Emily had a strong desire for autonomic control of her body.

Katherine Frank concludes that Emily Brontë's anorexia was a response to her Victorian repressive household, in which "she seized control of the only thing which was malleable: her own body" (5), but Frank rejects the possibility of a reading of Brontë's asceticism within the context of mysticism (4). Nevertheless, Emily Brontë can be placed in the context of female mystics, whose fasting and visions, according to Carolyn Walker Bynum, "led women to an acquisition of power in the world while affirming their knowledge of themselves as women. Visions were a socially sanctioned activity that freed a woman from conventional female roles by identifying her as a genuine religious figure" (*Jesus as Mother* 172).

Brontë, then, not only attempted a reclaiming of the body, but seen within the context of the mystics, she led the life of a socially unsanctioned "seer," an unconventional mystic, who rejected the boundaries of the male views of spirituality and nature, preferring instead a female-defined poetic sphere of stars and Gothic imagery, much like Emily Dickinson.

Brontë embraces the "world within" as a "brightness" of imagination that exists happily where "all around / danger and grief and darkness lie," in "To Imagination" (205–6). Resisting food, resisting the outer world, Emily Brontë stands as a character not unlike those found in Victorian children's literature by critic Jacqueline P. Banerjee, who finds "strong characters, who speak to us so urgently of the need for courage and resistance, and who certainly leave a mark on those around them (as well as on us, the readers), [but who] fail to relate successfully to society at large" (492).

The Victorian home was a difficult one for children like Emily Brontë, who was, if not exploited, certainly excluded from a healthy social life. Brontë biographers have long commented upon the bizarre Brontë home. John Maynard freely advances the thought that "[w]e can read, if we like, incest patterns, lesbian or heterosexual, into the relations of Anne, Emily, Branwell, and Charlotte, in any combination our fancy chooses" (12). Indeed, a number of biographers have advanced diverse theories on Emily's sexuality, many of these being essentialist phallocentric reductions of Emily's supposed wish to be a man.

Regardless of whether we assume Emily had incestuous desires for her siblings or lesbian desires for Ellen Nussey, as Jeannette Foster has suggested (132, 133), the home life of Emily Brontë was ruled over by the fearsome figure of the Reverend Patrick Brontë. He is described as bitter, abusive, and demanding in Katherine Frank's biography. Frank describes an unforgettable incident in which Patrick Brontë burned the boots of the Brontë children, who had set out for a walk on the moors (33).

This willful display of sadism, of control over the behavior of the children, was underscored by the reverend's manner of beginning the day "with an ear-piercing pistol shot and a bullet sailing" (Frank 9) from his bedroom window. These incidences suggest a pattern of psychologically, if not physically abusive, behavior—an environment that ironically forced the Brontë children to find "a symbolic mode in which to develop a relatively open discussion of passion," as Maynard observes (13), in their furtive yet empowering act of writing.

In "Stars," a male figure interrupts the fantasy world with a violent display of corporeal power, quite in keeping with the reverend's daily aural exhibition of the male capability of violence. The pistol shot of the Brontë patriarch is as physically oppressive as the gaze of the phallic sun, which assaults the loving "Stars," or female figures, involved in a romantic embrace: "Blood-red he rose, and arrow straight / His fierce beams struck my brow" (226).

Though Margaret Homans has difficulty arriving at a distinct gendered interpretation of the stars, and she correctly observes "that nowhere is it indicated that they are masculine" (158), she suggests the possibility that stars and night might be "feminine and maternal" (158). Textual evidence places Nature, Earth, and Sun imagery as male and oppressive. Thus, a diametric opposition is formed against the Stars and Night, female symbols in sexual union. "All through the night" [the stars] "glorious eyes / were gazing down in mine" prior to the violent intrusion of the sun.

Brontë describes the loving stars "at peace" and uses a food-related metaphor to explain how the central narrator "drank" the "beams / as if they were life to me," in a display of the sharing of food and sexual fluids between the bodies of female figures. This metaphor is tied to the "dew" alluded to in the final stanza, another female sexual metaphor. It is followed more immediately with the image of the sea, a water image firmly associated with the feminine body. It is important that the "changeful dreams / like petrel on the sea," imply both sexual and intellectual union in the next stanza:

> Thought followed thought—star followed star
> Through boundless regions on,
> While one sweet influence, near and far,
> Thrilled through and proved us one.
>
> (225–26)

Lillian Faderman reminds us that lesbian love does not require a "genital component" (37). In Faderman's view, critics are unwilling to view sexuality as anything less than a sexual act and are "unwilling to give [lesbian love] the dimensions they might attribute to a serious male-female love relationship" (37). The "boundless regions" of "Stars" suggests a heaven of sisterly sexual communion, of oneness between women.

Emily Brontë's preference for the female, combined with her lush metaphors of the beauty of the feminine, reveals a conspicuous desire for an ordered universe in which female or lesbian love can be expressed and consummated. Emily may have been writing her desire for incestuous female love through a complex use of gendered metaphors. Brontë's female *prosopopeic* retreat in "Stars" bespeaks her irrepressible fantasies, which are only disrupted by male violence.

Nancy Armstrong sees how Brontë "took issue with a public opinion that suppressed certain kinds of fantasy in order to sanction others as realistic" ("Emily Brontë" 257). Armstrong notes that the use of violence in *Wuthering Heights* is a way of "making something new of" [the usual] "division of the semantic universe into parlor and heath, male and female, past and present, real and fictive" (258). The insufferable surveillance of women within the Victorian household breeds an atmosphere in which violent outbreaks could almost be seen as inevitable within women's fiction.

Brontë repeatedly uses the metaphor of the wound in "Stars," for example, when sun scorches stars. Wounding is a metaphor frequently seen in male poetry in which the heart is wounded in a traditional analogy of sexual penetration. Significantly, Brontë reinscribes the metaphoric site of penetration. Here, the "arrow" pierces the "brow" of the narrator of the poem. That it does not pierce the heart, the usual site of wounding, suggests that Brontë specifically alludes to the mental capacity of the female creative figure, who is wounded by the male "Blood-red" fatherly figure. This reinscription of a traditional poetic usage of the wound suggests Brontë's capabilities of writing a distinctly feminized order in which female creative powers are constructed as both sexual and cognitive.

That the Brontë children were not given paper to write upon, were strictly forced to undergo a life of "proper" moral guidance, and were forced to work under extremely furtive circumstances sheds biographical support for such a reading. Indeed, the arrow strikes down the writer/ lover engaged in the pleasures of the body and psyche and remains in the same room in a threatening posture throughout the poem. This male intrusionary figure breaks the "pure" "spell" being enjoyed by the feminine figure(s) and imprisons them. The narrator asks:

> Why did the morning rise to break
> So great, so pure a spell,
> And scorch with fire the tranquil cheek
> Where your cool radiance fell?

(226)

It is important to note Brontë's use of temporal flow. The narrator, Brontë's other, whose soul "sank sad and low!" attempts to reclaim her previous activities through a lengthy and stressful denial of the presence of the sun, but even with her "lids closed down," she sees "him blazing still" (226). Next, she laments that even by burying her face in her pillow, she cannot escape the vampiric imprisoner:

> I turned me to the pillow then
> To call back Night, and see
> Your worlds of solemn light, again
> Throb with my heart and me!
>
> (226)

Brontë's *prosopopeia* barely masks the probability that Brontë is rerendering her own Victorian home in distinctively phantasmagoric imagery. The passage of time in the poem is painful and anxiety filled:

> It would not do—the pillow glowed
> And glowed both roof and floor,
> And birds sang loudly in the wood,
> And fresh winds shook the door.
>
> (226)

Here Brontë describes a nightmarish daylit prison inescapably reminiscent of Tennyson's "Mariana." Brontë's bedchamber becomes truly horrific to the narrator:

> The curtains waived, the wakened flies
> Were murmuring around my room.
>
> (226)

In Tennyson's "Mariana" (1830), the bizarre mental state of the central female narrator experiences strikingly similar images of a ghastly home in which "white curtains" sway "to and fro" and "wild winds" erupt (7). Ironically, in this male poet's vision of an imprisoned female, it is the lack of a male presence that ostensibly causes the horror of the female figure. Brontë's version reverses this paradigm: it is the presence of the male figure that causes the interruption of female bliss and solitude. Unlike Mariana, Brontë's female figure does not succumb to the power of the psychological violence. Instead, she willfully calls to her Night and Stars, imploring them to "hide me from the hostile light / That does not warm, but burn" (226).

Brontë's insistence in the constancy of the burning light of the vampirish sun "That drains the blood of suffering men" is an exemplification of fear of the familial male authoritarian figure. Elisabeth Bronfen describes these "animated corpses preserved in the dangerous liminal realm, as moments of failed decomposition" (295). Additionally, the nineteenth-century versions of the vampire, (the undead) were considered a "potential source of danger because death is thought to come from the body" (296).

Thus, the final cry of the narrator in "Stars," "Let me sleep through his blinding reign, / And only wake with you!" (227), reclaims the earlier site of the loving and thinking female bodies in blissful "boundless regions" of freedom, even while the constancy of the dangerous male gaze of the vampire continues to be a source of death to female creativity. Brontë's sleep deprivation provides a context to view her attitude toward the vampires that invade her bedchamber in "Stars," and elsewhere throughout her poetry. In 1837, she wrote a harrowing poem, "Sleep brings no joy to me," in which "the shadows of the dead" surround her bed (54), and "They all gaze, oh how scornfully" (55).

Vampires appear again in "Remembrance" (1845), but here they are associated specifically with learned deprivation. Brontë probably alludes to her dead sisters and mother: "All my life's bliss is in the grave with thee" (223), but the narrator sternly resolves, "Then did I learn how existence could be cherished, / strengthened and fed without the aid of joy" (223). In 1845, Brontë specified feminine spirits that sustain her ("she lulls my pain for others' woe" [232]). She summons the female, asking, "My guide, sustained by thee?" (233). In "Stars," Brontë questions why the feminine body must depart, leaving her in the company of the vampiric male sun figure.

Anne K. Mellor observes that Emily Brontë was aware of the extent that the "body determines one's options: to die—and thus enable the ultimate triumph of the body, the reabsorption of the self into nature—or to live and be socially constructed as a woman—a daughter, sister, wife or mother—and hence a dependent on patriarchal power" (208). The imprisoned female body is at the center of Brontë's poetic sphere, as it is in the work of Emily Dickinson. "The dungeon is for both poets the paradoxical double," writes Erkila (63). It is freeing, in that it shields the female body from the male world, but it is also "an emblem of female entrapment" (63).

In "Stars" and elsewhere in her poetry, Brontë battles with the Nature she associated with the patriarchal, but she embraced the darker side of Nature, the female night world in which her imagination ruled over the world of the Gondals. As Gondal's queen, she freely reigned imaginatively over her own metaphoric body and quite often the imprisoned male bodies. Nina Auerbach concludes, "The saga of its queen and the silence of its creator suggest that this gaunt woman who wanted never to leave her father's parsonage was a braver navigator into the straights of time and change than the sterner more sonorous bards whose poetry constituted her age's official voice" (229).

If we can read the poetry of Emily Brontë as a "performed act," an act of an other, we can glimpse the buried life of Emily Brontë, whose written work and asceticism must have provided some form of catharsis. The sustained effort of her work over the period of her lifetime would support this reading, and perhaps we can even ascertain that Emily Brontë experienced some of the *jouissance* associated with female writing. Even as she hid her self and starved herself, Brontë could not finally overtake her need to perform herself as a being and a spirit in conflict with Victorian constructions of the female self.

"Stars" betrays a poetic voice of a female who attempts to reclaim her body through the metaphors of feasting on the feminine. Her opening cry is all the more compelling if it is read as a rejection of the possibility of a reunion of the male and female spheres of Sun and Stars.

> Ah! why, because the dazzling sun
> Restored my earth to joy
> Have you departed, every one,
> And left a desert sky?

(225)

As a subtext, the narrator, read as the poet, can be read as a fragmented or disarticulated self calling out to her own denied sexual body, attempting a cathartic performance of the "male" and "female" sides of Emily's *prosopopeiac*, or masked bodies which were unable to coexist in the confines of Victorian sexuality.

Brontë continues to reclaim her repressed "grotesque" body and obstinately defies us in our continual reassessment of her work. Her Gondal poems stand as indecipherable, yet we stand and drink her beams of glorious female ludicity "with a full heart's thankful sighs" (845). They remind us again of Cixous' words: "A feminine text cannot fail to be more than subversive. It is volcanic; as it is written it brings about an upheaval of the old property crust, carrier of masculine investments; there is no other way" (888).

In this context, Emily Brontë can be placed in context with lesbian poets Katherine Bradley and Edith Cooper, who wrote under the pen name of Michael Field. Angela Leighton notes how Michael Field in "Embalmment" subverts the figure of woman's repressed sexuality, "a sexuality that only flowers in the grave—and turned it into a figure of . . . live and 'rapid' responsiveness" (236):

> Let not a star suspect the mystery!
> A cave that haunts thee in dreams of night
> Keep me as treasure hidden from thy sight,
> And only thine while thou dost covet me!
> As the Asmonaean queen perpetually

Embalmed in honey, cold to thy delight,
Cold to thy touch, a sleeping eremite,
Beside thee never sleeping I would be.

(qtd. in Leighton 235)

Emily Brontë's sexuality would remain primarily buried in metaphors, even as it expressed itself in her willful displays of sleep and food deprivation. Nevertheless, textual evidence suggests that Emily Brontë experienced an inner psychic state of bliss, reminiscent of the visions of female medieval mystics. In "Sleep Brings No Joy to Me" (1837), Brontë alludes to her "harassed heart" (55), but she transforms the negative experience of this harassed heart into a positive one in an untitled poem of 1838:

A little while, a little while,
The noisy crowd are barred away;
And I can sing and I can smile
A little while I've holyday!
Where wilt thou go, my harassed heart?
Full many a land invites thee now;
And places near and far apart
Have rest for thee my weary brow.

(93–94)

Brontë transports her "harassed heart" to a landscape that metaphorically reinscribes the vaginal cavity as an environmental womb of desire:

The mute bird sitting on the stone,
The dank moss dripping from the wall,
The garden-walk with weeds o'ergrown,
I love them all—how I love them all!

(94)

She imagines an even loftier realm in her "naked room" where images of mountains describe a female body in a state of jouissance:

A little on a lone green lane
That opened on a common wide;
A distant, dreamy, dim blue chain
Of mountains circling every side;
A heaven so clear, an earth so calm,
So sweet, so soft, so hushed an air
And, deepening still the dream-like charm,
Wild moor-sheep feeding everywhere—

(95)

Once again, Brontë's mystical experience, her female sensual haven, is disrupted by physical reality. The narrator claims she "could have lingered but a hour . . . but truth has banished fancy's power," as she hears "my dungeon bars recoil—" (95). The oenic imagery of dank moss, an overgrown garden walk, and enclosing mountains are sensuous female metaphors of a disassociated female body in a state of visionary status that calms the "harassed heart." Even as the dungeon bars of patriarchal reality recoil upon the narrator, she continues to attempt to enjoy the mystical/sexual experience:

> Even as I stood with raptured eye
> Absorbed in bliss so deep and dear
> My hour of rest had fleeted by
> And given me back to weary care.
>
> (95)

In her anorexic state of seeking to become an other, Brontë was quite capable of disassociation from her body. Brontë's untitled poem of 1839 begins:

> It is not pride, it is not shame;
> That makes her leave the gorgeous hall;
> And though neglect her heart might tame
> She mourns not for her sudden fall.
>
> (124)

Here, Brontë self-reflexively addresses her own denial of food. What makes Emily deny food, or leave the gorgeous hall, she tells us, isn't a mere emotional response, such as pride or shame, nor is it religious piousness. The narrative point of view of the poem is in fact the cry of a disassociated self in search of the body reclaimed:

> 'Tis true she stands among the crowd
> An unmarked and an unloved child,
> While each young comrade, blithe and proud,
> Glides through the maze of pleasure wild.
>
> (124)

Brontë guides us on a quest to unmask the othered female self, inviting us to ask with her:

> What made her weep, what made her glide
> Out to the park this dreary day,
> And cast her jewelled chains aside,
> And seek a rough and lonely way,
>
> (124)

The next stanza hints at a possible interpretation of asceticism as a form of religion of the self for Brontë:

> And down beneath a cedar's shade
> On the wet grass regardless lie,
> With nothing but its gloomy head
> Between her and the showery sky?
>
> (124–25)

Brontë's mysticism is an experience of the self outside of the boundaries of the "jewelled chains" of familial imprisonment. She is at one with herself. She is unmasked. Brontë completes the embrace of the self, re-united with the physical, her body "on the wet grass regardless" in an experience of pure physical delight. Brontë closes the poem with a final contemplation of the self. She sees her masked self:

> I saw her standing in the gallery long,
> Watching the little children there,
> As they were playing the pillars among
> And bounding down the marble stair.
>
> (125)

Brontë is at work here fashioning an empowered female body. In doing this, she was not only attempting to embrace her own body, but she was at war with the contemporary patriarchal and clerical definitions of the female body. She metaphorically disassociates her self from the patriarchal surveillance of her own body by performing an act of self-surveillance. Brontë recreates the war she had with her own body. Even in the confines of her ludic creative zones, she cannot enter into play with these children/her selves.

Brontë not only refused food and sleep, but she refused to behave in the manner specified by her father and society. Unlike her sister, Charlotte, she refused to take up the life of a teacher. She refused the ideals of courtship; she denied the primacy of her father's church and in every way displayed her dissatisfaction with the role of the Victorian woman. Brontë's behavior does not seem at all bizarre in comparison with that of some of the female mystics whose asceticism included self-flagellation and other grotesque behavior. Both the medieval women mystics and Emily Brontë sought to empower the female self through a union of the "grotesque" and "classical" selves, but Emily had another agenda, the poetic transmission of a repressed homosexual nature that could not, apparently, remain completely repressed.

The themes of lesbian love, vampirish incest, and imprisonment in "Stars" and other Brontë poetry convey a lesbian literary imagination. Hence, Brontë's refiguring of the mystical experience is directly connected to her lesbian sense of herself and her body. Brontë then takes herself hostage and denies the pleasure of the male imprisoner, her father, the Sun and the Holy "All-Seeing Eyed" father.

Emily Brontë's poetry corresponds with that of other female poets in that it speaks of a distinctly feminine quest for reuniting female bodies and for a feminine language of self-representation that is complicated by a desire to remain hidden. The gap between the representation of Emily Brontë as secretive, childlike, and madly anorexic and Emily Brontë as poetess and creator of an entire matriarchal universe is the gap of the feminine writer. Emily Brontë dreamt of a female oneness that bespeaks the desire to reclaim the female body and a language of female desire. Brontë was successful in her own right, in both her poetry and her fiction, in reclaiming the feminine. She was equally successful in denying the masculine hegemony the right to dominate her body or her desires. She ignored their rules and made her own, even if she deprived her body of the pleasures of the corpus. In her denial of food and sleep, Brontë positioned herself as an instrument of divine self-will. Like many feminist poets, she regenders and rearticulates the body of Christ as the body of the female poet. She meditates on the female body and drinks the beam of feminine desire.

7

Regendering the Romantics: Renarrative Techniques of Victorian Conduct Writers

> We are eager for improvement in politics, in education, even in morals, though in this last our idea of improvement chiefly consists in persuading or forcing other people to be as good as ourselves. . . . It is individuality that we war against.
>
> —John Stuart Mill, *On Liberty*

Popular writers of Victorian etiquette and conduct books responded to a society eager for instruction and guidance. The atmosphere of uncertainty present in the mid-nineteenth century in Britain and the United States provided an environment conducive to uniformity and propaganda. In the United States, factors such as the end of the Civil War, the economic climate, growing population, social mobility, and increasing philosophical conflicts provided the optimum "malleable environment" for the dissemination and fertilization of propaganda (Ellul 92).

The work of romantic poets, especially Wordsworth, is frequently cited in the Victorian era conduct books, which are clearly a response to social anxieties. Read within this contextual framework, the ideology and aesthetic of Wordsworth is neatly adapted to suit the purposes of the Victorians. Analyzing these acts of ideological subversion, it becomes clear that propagandistic literary techniques are employed to limit, tame, and defuse the meanings of the original material.

Late-nineteenth-century American etiquette books reflect an American preoccupation with social refinement, and, as others have noted, they "represent the British mid-Victorian attitude, not the American" (Markun 581), so it is not surprising to see British poets liberally spicing up American conduct books. Here they are joined by presidents, philosophers, Scripture, and a host of figures appropriated for their authoritative "stamp of approval"—a bandwagon of voices that appear to support the concrete tropes of "good" behavior in all its ideological bases.

The primary work is not simply appropriated or reassessed, but recontextualized and "renarrated" (defined as a process through which one may identify "the tale that the overt [narrative] prevents [from] being told" [Zavarzadeh 19]) to suit the propaganda of instructional literature. Just as literary voices "mutate" in the critical feast, the voice of Wordsworth suffers from misquotation, the chopping-up of descriptive passages, omissions, and a whole range of renarrative appropriating strategies. Thus dismembered and reconstituted, Wordsworth's poetry is often reduced to the level of cliché and platitude we expect to find in the didactic literature of conduct.

The typical Victorian reader of instructional texts sought an emotionally fulfilling "Utopian" narrative, a requiting "quest for a lost unity of body and soul" (Flynn 73). How ironic, then, that this quest is similar to the journey on which Wordsworth so often embarks. The problem arises when the utopian models of the ideology of the poet are diametrically opposed to those of the Victorian conduct writer. The poet's words become hostages to texts that seek a utopian conformity in everything from women's conduct to business behavior.

One of the more interesting renarrations of Wordsworth comes as a result of the changing of gender expectations in the Victorian era. In John Ruskin's conduct book for women, *Pearls for Young Ladies*, Ruskin's renarrated version of Wordsworth's "Three Years She Grew" (from *Poems of the Imagination*) appears in a chapter on "What Kind of Education Is to Fit a Woman for Her Sphere?" Ruskin disregards the political or philosophical themes of Wordsworth's elegiac poem, in an attempt to metaphorically bring to life an objectified vision of the female.

Wordsworth's original text is this:

> Three years she grew in sun and shower,
> Then Nature said, "A lovelier flower
> On earth was never sown;
> This Child I to myself will take;
> She shall be mine, and I will make
> A Lady of my own.
>
> "Myself will to my darling be
> Both law and impulse: and with me
> The Girl, in rock and plain,
> In earth and heaven, in glade and bower,

Shall feel an overseeing power
To kindle or restrain

"She shall be sportive as the fawn
That wild with glee across the lawn
Or up the mountain springs;
And her's shall be the breathing balm,
And her's the silence and the calm
Of mute insensate things.

"The floating clouds their state shall lend
To her: for her the willow bend;
Nor shall she fail to see
Even in the motions of the Storm
Grace that shall mould the Maiden's form
By silent sympathy.

"The stars of midnight shall be dear
To her; and she shall lean her ear
In many a secret place
Where rivulets dance their wayward round,
And beauty born of murmuring sound
Shall pass into her face.

"And vital feelings of delight
Shall rear her form to stately height
Her virgin bosom swell;
Such thoughts to Lucy I will give
While she and I together live
Here in this happy dell."

Ruskin completely omits the final six lines in which:

Thus nature spake—The Work was done—
How soon my Lucy's race was run!
She died, and left to me
This heath, this calm, and quiet scene;
The memory of what has been
And never more will be.

(*Poetical Works* 2: 214–16)

Thus, Ruskin's version of "Three Years She Grew" emphasizes the description of Lucy as an embodiment of his view of the "*right*ness" of feminine beauty, as if offering advice for the female reader looking for fashion counsel "Fit for a Woman of Her Sphere." The sensibility with which Wordsworth renders his female character is replaced with a clearly purposeful redefinition of Lucy as object. Wordsworth's voice in the poem is renarrated by Ruskin, and the result is a new construct that bears little resemblance to the contextualized image.

Missing is Wordsworth's characteristic concern with the tension between the specificity of an individual character and the universality of a phenomenon like death; in Ruskin's hands, Lucy becomes simply an objectified, unattributed example. Lucy is thus applied to the utopic model of female behavior in Victorian society. This renarration of "Three Years She Grew" reveals a central tendency of Victorian gender definition.

Timothy Titcomb [Josiah Gilbert Holland], like John Ruskin, appropriates Wordsworth's female figure in his misogynist text, *Titcomb's Letters to Young People Single and Married*. In a chapter entitled "Dress— Its Proprieties and Abuses," Titcomb quotes a few selected words from Wordsworth and uses them to convey an objectifying stance toward women. Wordsworth is renarrated to sound as though he supports the embrace of the Victorian model of womanhood or the ornamental fixture: "A perfect woman, nobly planned / To warm, to comfort, and command" (85). The "systematic depreciation of the feminine" (Richardson 14), which Alan Richardson finds in the Victorian period, accounts in part for the compulsive renarration of Wordsworth's female.

Also important to note is the fact that in Ruskin's appropriation of "Three Years She Grew," Wordsworth is left unnamed. He is referred to as "that poet who is distinguished . . . by exquisite *right*ness" (44). Robbed of any vestige of his authorial identity, Wordsworth's vision takes a backseat to Ruskin's. Clearly, Ruskin appreciates and respects Wordsworth, but he is still willing to appropriate him freely. Ruskin's appropriation of Wordsworth's authority and work is part of a larger popular movement to integrate early nineteenth century thought into the later nineteenth century.

Wordsworth is commonly cited by social manner makers of the period, partly owing to his growing popularity. The romantics are chosen by these later writers and compilers for the beauty of their language and their arguments for the cause of social responsibility. The latter is a requisite for the conduct industry. As literary figures of the past, they add authorial power to the otherwise banal texts, and they provide an ideological bridge between the romantic and Victorian philosophies and religious views about the self in society.

Carl Woodring has noted that emphasis on "both the individual and a kind of collectivism . . . were present in the Romantic movement" (39). Woodring traces the authority of the Romantics through their access to classical education, and ultimately to their familiarity with the Old Testament, concluding that it was "from this moral base that [the] poets rose to prophesy" (45). The Romantic tension between an emphasis on individuality and sociability is replaced by the Victorians' vision of the group.

In *Titcomb's Letters to Young People Single and Married*, Wordsworth's authority is spent on a text concerning the "Social Duties and Privileges": "The primal duties shine aloft like stars, / The Charities that soothe, and heal, and bless, / Are scatter'd at the feet of man like flowers" (62). With these words in mind, Titcomb admonishes the reader to "get hold of the idea that they are members of a society" (62). Poetic text is simplified, homogenized, and rendered politically harmless here. These same words, in their original context and entirety (or within the larger context of the poet's total body of work), may be read as politically subversive calls to action. Certainly, Wordsworth wrote in favor of community obligation, but he readily expressed contempt for pre-established codes of mannerly behavior, deeming them oppositional to the forces of his Nature, labeling "misguided and misguiding . . . all precepts, judgments, maxims, creeds" in *The Prelude* (1850, 11. 293–94).

In another conduct text, C. H. Payne's *Guides and Guards in Character Building* (1883), Wordsworth's view of the self is used to support the Victorian ideology of repression of the self. In *Guides and Guards in Character Building*, Wordsworth's poem *"Lines Left upon a Seat in a Yew-Tree"* (from the poet's series *Descriptive Sketches*) is cited at the top of a chapter entitled "Self-Respect and Self-Control (340)":

> True dignity abides with him alone
> Who, in the silent hour of inward thought,
> Can still suspect and still revere himself
> In lowliness of heart.
>
> (*Poetical Works* 1: 94)

Recontextualized in a distinctly religious-utopic model, Wordsworth's philosophy of the self is renarrated within the discourse of utilitarian thought. Wordsworth becomes a Victorian voice calling for order in society.

The major Romantics are routinely exhumed and renarrated for such "quaint" tomes as *Written for You, or, The Art of Beautiful Living*, whose anonymous contributors provide, as editor "Mrs. M. L. Rayne" promises in the title, *A Large Amount of Valuable Knowledge Concerning the Every-Day Affairs of Life, Social Propriety, Mental and Moral Culture, and All That Pertains to the Successful Realization of a True and Beautiful Life*. Rayne's essayists cite strategic fragments of poetry to anchor their "philosophy" in the authority of writers as diverse as Shakespeare, Milton, Christina Rossetti, and Leigh Hunt in this beautifully bound and illustrated Victorian artifact.

Wordsworth is enlisted by Rayne's contributors as an example of a "religious moralist" (84). Wordsworth's lines from "Ode: Intimations of Immortality": "But trailing clouds of glory do we come / From God who is our home: / Heaven lies about us in our infancy!" are thus made to support the religious position adopted by Rayne's text (*Poetical Works* 4: 281). Wordsworth, who places spirituality squarely in the natural landscape in "Places of Worship" from his series "Ecclesiastical Sonnets" with the following lines would scarcely have declared himself, even in his older conservative days, as a "religious moralist" as defined in Rayne's conduct manual:

> Her spires, her Steeple-towers with glittering vanes
> Far-kenned, her Chapels lurking among trees,
> Where a few villagers on bended knees
> Find solace which a busy world disdains.
>
> (*Poetical Works* 3: 392)

In another moralizing renarration, the Reverend Henry Ward Beecher's *Addresses to Young Men* (1895) manages to completely rewrite Wordsworth's "I Wandered Lonely as a Cloud" as a religious parable. In Wordsworth's poem, the second stanza contains these words:

> Continuous as the stars that shine
> And twinkle on the milky way,
> They stretched in never-ending line
> Along the margin of a bay:
> Ten thousand saw I at a glance,
> Tossing their heads in sprightly dance.
>
> (*Poetical Works* 2: 216)

Beecher transforms Wordsworth's text into a phantasmal admonition: "[T]here are in the clouds ten thousand inimitable forms and hues to be found nowhere else / Ten thousand eyes stare full upon these things and see nothing; and yet the Divine artist has finished his matchless work" (Beecher 105–6). Beecher neither credits the poet nor quotes the poem accurately. He renders Wordsworth's ten thousand daffodils as a blind, useless, and sublimated crowd. In Beecher's renarration, the poet and the people are sublimated by the all-seeing, all-creating God, and nature is duly rewritten as a landscape of creationism. The poet's utterance is reworked to support the ideology of blind and unquestioning obedience to the church.

Nature is rationalized, ordered, and domesticated in the chapter "Favorite Flowers" in Rayne's anthology. Here we are offered a poetic greenhouse, laden with descriptive passages on flowers, bereft of the Romantics' intended political implications and themes of human loss and regeneration. Wordsworth is at once renarrated in terms of both nature and the female body. Wordsworth's "Two April Mornings" is renamed as "Cinquefoil—The Beloved Child" (433). One might argue that Rayne chose this particular stanza for its signification of the feminine in an ornamental objectified state of death:

> Six feet in earth my Emma lay;
> And yet I loved her more,
> For so it seemed, than till the day
> I e'er had loved before.
>
> (*Poetical Works* 4: 70)

Many critics have noted the Victorian preoccupation with the dead, or near dead, female body as it represented a "safe" sexual state of passivity of the female body.

Wendell Harris finds that critics "who looked to the moral development of the individual . . . celebrated Wordsworth, [while] those who required the improvement of the social structure . . . through reason . . . were dubious" (468). The Victorian conduct writer is certainly "dubious" but poses as being celebratory of Wordsworth and other Romantics. When short, carefully chosen passages of *The Prelude*, for example, are used to illustrate simplistic platitudes of moral persuasion, it has the "fragmentary effect of illuminating only a corner here, a column there" (W. Harris 464). A few lines from Wordsworth's "Hart-Leap Well" thus are made to appear to support religious orthodoxy and decorum, as renarrated in Walter T. Griffin's *The Homes of Our Country, or the Centers of Moral and Religious Influence*. Griffin states that "Wordsworth has well expressed one of the cardinal rules of politeness in the admonition" (326) and then cites two lines from the poem: "never to blend our pleasure and our pride / With sorrow to the meanest thing that feels" (*Poetical Works* 2: 254). Perhaps Wordsworth might well have selected the following example from "The Tables Turned" as an antidote, expressing to Griffin's appropriation his preference for nature's law over human artifice:

> One impulse from a vernal wood
> May teach you more of man,
> Of moral evil and of good,
> Than all the sages can.
>
> (*Poetical Works* 4: 57)

William Marshall's *Nature as a Book of Symbols* is designed to show the "whole universe to be a moral unity" (xiv). Although this statement sounds in keeping with Wordsworth's "one life," Wordsworth is found to be spiritually lacking by this author: "Wordsworth—who was emphatically the poet of Nature,—was well acquainted with her beautiful face and ever-changing features, and at times had communion with her mind, but he scarcely ever had a glimpse into her Spirit, and has therefore failed to make her a medium of lofty spiritual instruction, and a means of great moral uplifting to mankind" (Marshall 80–81).

Here we see an instance in which a popular Victorian writer attacks Wordsworth's masculine capabilities, defining Nature as a feminine force whom the poet supposedly cannot sexually conquer. Since Wordsworth cannot "make her" an agency of moral instruction, the poet is emasculated and seen as a failure. "Successful" poets for Marshall are those who "accurately" portray Scripture (e.g., Tennyson and Whittier [Marshall 81]). In a stunning act of cultural displacement, Marshall combines the first and fourth stanzas of "Lines Written in Early Spring," lauding Wordsworth's ability to be "cheered by the songs of the birds" (208). Marshall's bowdlerized version carefully omits the poet's critique of "what man has made of man," rendering the poem useful as an exercise in Christian "symbolism":

> I heard a thousand blended notes,
> While in a grove I sate reclined,
> In that sweet mood when pleasant thoughts
> Bring sad thoughts to mind.
>
> The birds around me hopped and played,
> Their thoughts I cannot measure:—
> But the least motion which they made,
> It seem'd a thrill of pleasure.
>
> (208)

The missing lines reveal Wordsworth's intent:

> To her fair works did Nature link
> The human soul that through me ran;
> And much it grieved my heart to think
> What man has made of man.
>
> Through primrose tufts, in that green bower,
> The periwinkle trailed its wreaths;
> And 'tis my faith that every flower
> Enjoys the air it breathes.
>
> (*Poetical Works* 4: 58)

Laurence Lockridge reads two of the lines omitted by Marshall ("Tis my faith that every flower / Enjoys the air it breathes") as an example of the "hedonistic element of Romanticism" evident in Wordsworth (132).

Hedonism stands at odds with the values of Victorian conduct writers. Perhaps a reading of "Tintern Abbey" by a Victorian professor of aesthetics gives a ready assessment of the moral climate of the times as they permeated all aspects of social existence, even in academe. In *Poetry as a Representative Art*, George Lansing Raymond finds "Tintern Abbey" to be a celebration of "the universal and divine love manifested in the form of Christ" (346), a rather limited interpretation of a poem that has been cited in many differing philosophical critical arguments.

Within the utilitarian model of Victorian popular thinking, poets find their true "place" within the landscape of commerce. Thomas E. Hill's *Manual of Social and Business Forms* (1891) is a perfect example of the "practical" Victorian use of the Romantic vision. The title of this massive reference volume tells a great deal about the content and style of the work, as well as of the increasing importance of commerce in all areas of Victorian society. Codes of etiquette are referred to as "laws," which are presumably policed, and whose disregard results in economic failure. Significantly, "Writing Poetry" comes last in Hill's compendium of topics and is listed as a social or business skill, rather than as an artistic profession.

The mercantile "place" of poetry within Hill's Victorian world can be judged from a series of informational "tables" in the volume; it is certainly no accident that Hill lists the "Poets Laureate of England," from Spenser to Tennyson, directly beside a detailed list of the "Number of Horses and Cattle in the Principal Countries of the World." It is also of interest to note that, in his table of the "Poets Laureate," Hill briefly describes each writer; for Wordsworth, Hill notes that he "wrote little that is generally known" (303).

Another business guide from the Victorian era, William O. King's *Portraits and Principles of the World's Great Men and Women* (1896), includes a compilation of essays by "great thinkers," with emphasis on commercial success and social practicality. This volume appropriates the lives, rather than the words, of the romantic poets. Thus, Wordsworth is seen primarily as a successful businessman, who made shrewd publishing deals, pursued his debtors in courts, and "received a government office worth $4,000 a year" (King 510). For King, then, the life of a poet is reduced to terms of the marketplace. The poet's career is a commodity not any different than that of a banker.

Wordsworth's poetry undergoes an ideological dismemberment in the works of Victorian conduct literature. His authority usurped, he is made to mouth the ideology of an age quite different from his own. His metaphors are presented as flat, "representational," and decorative. His female figures are refigured into the rhetoric of the growing policy of separate spheres. His views on nature, the individual, and the language of the poet are made to conform to a utopic Victorian world view. Most distressing, though, is the manner in which Wordsworth is commodified as poet and authority in the increasingly utilitarian ideology of the marketplace.

The Victorian conduct writers' attempt to appropriate and renarrate the works of William Wordsworth for their own ends failed because it was, in the end, dishonest, and of course because their ideology was superseded. Selective quotation, textual displacement, and direct misinterpretation were just a few of the tools they employed in their attempts to usurp the authority of Wordsworth. If we hold with Blake that "the Grandest Poetry is Immoral the Grandest Characters Wicked" (633–34), then any attempt to bend the vision of these poets to extrinsic purposes of "moral instruction" is obviously fore-doomed. The proof of this is the resilience of the works of the romantic poets. The texts of the Victorian conduct writers survive only to remind us of the rigid conformity of the era.

8

The Performing Body in Postmodern Conduct Narratives of Virginia Woolf and Edith Wharton

> A frivolous society can acquire dramatic significance only through what frivolity destroys. Its tragic implication lies in its power of debasing people and ideas.
>
> —Wharton on *The House of Mirth*

> In this book I have almost too many ideas. I want to give life and death, sanity and insanity, I want to criticize the social system and to show it at work, in its most intense.
>
> —Woolf on *Mrs. Dalloway*

Edith Wharton and Virginia Woolf shared a preoccupation with exposing the limitations of mannered societal codes of behavior that existed within the repressive Victorian society of their parents' generation. Candace Waid notes that Wharton was always "concerned with an opposition between truth and appearance" (10). Woolf exposed "society" as a "game," a dangerous yet frivolous game that elicited fragmentation of the self and humiliation of those who were not inclined to play. In *Moments of Being*, she described "society" as "the machine into which our bodies were inserted in 1900 [which] not only held us tight in its framework, but bit into us with innumerable sharp teeth" (152).

The "machine" described by Woolf suggests Michel Foucault's panopticon-modeled "disciplinary society," as described in *Discipline and Punish* (209). Wharton and Woolf articulated a world of "generalized surveillance" both in their descriptions of the experiences of their real "selves" and the fictionally inscribed "selves" of their characters. Woolf associated dances with "the humiliation of standing unpartnered" (*Moments* 155) and connected her "fragmentary feelings" (156) with the "battles" or "ordeals" of parties. Wharton remembered her teens with similarly disparaging remarks. Through the use of language, and attention to the performing bodies of Lily Bart and Clarissa Dalloway, Wharton and Woolf explore and reinscribe the troping of the female body as commodity, the arena of "society" as a performance of theatricality, and the fragmentation of the female self.

Wharton and Woolf articulate the modern self, defined by Anthony Giddens as "frail, brittle, fractured, fragmented . . . a conception probably the pre-eminent outlook in current discussions of the self and modernity" (169). The central characters in *The House of Mirth* and *Mrs. Dalloway*, Lily Bart and Clarissa Dalloway, not only are characterized by their own performance, words, and inner-speech but also are defined by the heteroglossic discourse of other characters. Bakhtin describes such characters as "character zones" or "zones formed from the fragments of character speech" (*Dialogic* 316). Julia Kristeva uses a similarly flexible terminology for a discussion of destabilized identities. Kristeva, recognizing that "the frontiers between differences of sex or identity, reality and fantasy, act and discourse, etc., are easily traversed," sees character zones as "as if" or "open structure personalities" (*Language* 9).

In a reading of the dominant characters of *The House of Mirth* and *Mrs. Dalloway*, then, it would be impossible to ignore how one character's speech and another's often merge. Bakhtin notes that the use of inner speech in the novel "permits another's inner speech to merge, in an organic and structured way, with a context belonging to the author" (*Dialogic* 319). Beth Newman describes this phenomena as an instance of free indirect discourse, which "disperses the narratorial look, distributing it across multiple focalizers" (1038). Both novelists playfully outwit those readers who insist upon rigidly defined characters and selves.

Wharton and Woolf embrace the borderlines of character zones or open structure identities and much of the depth and ambiguity of *The House of Mirth* and *Mrs. Dalloway* can be attributed to the realization of modernist strategies that defy simple readings of the "self" of Lily Bart or Mrs. Dalloway. Lily Bart is as much "fashioned" and "voiced" in her performed self and speaking self as she is by Lawrence Selden. Selden can be seen, then, as a fractured self or character zone of Lily Bart. It may be argued that all the characters in *Mrs. Dalloway* signify the disintegrated selves or character zones of Clarissa Dalloway, but for the sake of time, I will limit my readings to those selves who voice repressed desires of Clarissa Dalloway: Peter Walsh, Sally Seton, and Septimus Warren Smith.

Woolf's Mrs. Dalloway, the perfect hostess, is objectified, fragmented, and disciplined by exterior surveillance in much the same manner as

Wharton's Lily Bart, who readily adapts herself to the required mask of outward conduct, while refusing to conduct herself appropriately within the confines of repressive society. Mrs. Dalloway's painfully mannered party, then, juxtaposed with Lily Bart's famous *tableaux vivant* scene locates the female(s) in fragmented form as "disarticulated selves," as described by Ruth Porritt, who sees in Woolf an ability to use "multiple discourses or 'voices' to constitute meaning" (323). These selves exist in a world of supervision not unlike that described by Foucault as a prison-like reality of unwavering supervision and judgment, "a state of constant and permanent visibility" (*Discipline* 201), wherein the psychological manifestation ultimately leads to repressive self-surveillance.

In both *The House of Mirth* and *Mrs. Dalloway*, we are offered female characters who deny their "base" sexual impulses, displaying instead artificial performed bodies. In the case of Lily Bart, it is painfully obvious that she is physically attracted to a man who is not "proper marriage material," but it is in those moments of "forbidden height" (69) with Lawrence Selden that we first glimpse the sensual self, or the zone that is often referred to as "the real Lily Bart": "The soft isolation of the falling day enveloped them: they seemed lifted into a finer air. All the exquisite influences of the hour trembled in their veins, and drew them to each other as the loosened leaves were drawn to the earth" (69). Alas, society interjects itself just as the "adventurous children" embrace themselves. A sound "like the hum of a giant insect" (69) breaks up the coupling, and they will never consummate this type of unmannered natural love, at least within the boundaries of their physical life as performed in the fictive state.

But Wharton does not define Lily Bart's disintegrated selves in the expected straightforward manner of novelists of her time. Lily's relationship with Selden is secondary in importance compared with Lily's union with her own sexuality. The *tableaux vivant* scene, in which Lily makes a spectacle of herself, can be read as an almost masturbatory fantasy of self-wedding. Lily is dressed in a white gown, performing her fragmented selves in a public spectacle. She breaks with tradition and becomes a "self-creating artistic object," as Cynthia Griffin Wolff argues (110). Wharton indicts a society in which female self-love is not only taboo but a dangerous trope in opposition to male surveillance, discipline, and objectification of women in performance.

Virginia Woolf embeds another dangerous trope in Mrs. Dalloway, who is only at one with her fragmented selves in her fantasies of a lesbian sexual relationship. Lying in bed pondering the sexlessness of her marriage, Mrs. Dalloway reperforms the passionate charm of the female gaze of Sally Seton: "[O]nly for a moment; but it was enough. It was a sudden revelation, a tinge like a blush which one tried to check and then, as it spread, one yielded to its expansion, and rushed to the farthest verges and there quivered and felt the world come closer, swollen with some astonishing significance, some pressure of rapture, which split its thick skin and gushed and poured with an extraordinary alleviation over the cracks and sores! Then, for a moment, she had seen an illumination" (32). The language of the passage and the passage of time suggests a masturbatory fantasy, a performance of self-love not unlike Lily Bart's *tableaux vivant* of self-wedding and *jouissance*. Mrs. Dalloway's sexual reunion with her body is suddenly over, broken by the recognition of "the bed and Baron Morbot and the candle half-burnt," all evidences of a return to the world in which such fantasies are denied. The collective morality of the civilization in which Mrs. Dalloway is forced to repress her sexuality is reflective of the privatization of sexuality observed by Foucault in *The History of Sexuality:* "Sexuality was carefully confined: it moved into the home. The conjugal family took custody of it and absorbed it into the serious function of reproduction. On the subject of sex, silence became the rule . . . proper demeanor avoided contact with other bodies, and verbal decency sanitized one's speech" (3–4).

The unrepressed sexual selves of Mrs. Dalloway and Lily Bart constitute dangerous tropes of sex outside of reproductionary function. Both Virginia Woolf and Edith Wharton involve themselves with the societal attitude towards this dangerous trope, as it is manifested blatantly in their female characters. Society will continue to interject its boundaries like a giant insect intent upon preying on these suspect female figures. The disintegrated or fragmented selves of the female characters result from complete disallowal of self-defined sexual appetites in women in post-Victorian society. Woolf's embrace of the boundaries of self and sexuality suggests a character zone well described by Ban Wang: "It is a horizon where 'I' is on the run toward a space bereft of cultural constraints and linguistic shackles [and] . . . it is indeed Julia Kristeva's abject realm of imaginary darkness and chora" (189). Woolf and Wharton create character zones much like Kristevian projections of presocialized "chora," in which the body seems at once to struggle with external realities and symbolic immersion in "some great semiotic ocean," as suggested by Makiko Minow-Pinkney (163).

Ironically, Wharton was working on a novel to be titled *Disintegration* before she set to work on *The House of Mirth. The House of Mirth*, originally *A Moment's Ornament*, continually refers to the themes of fragmentation of self and the spectatorship of society. Wharton manipulates the narrative to suggest that the selves or character zones of Lily Bart and Lawrence Selden expand and contract, much like the flow of blood through human capillaries, throughout the novel. The letters that tear Selden and Lily apart merge their zones at the end of the novel. Lily has taken her own life, and Selden is trying to fathom his loss. He remembers her plea,

"When may I come to you?" (316). These words "overwhelm him," (316) and the selves of Lily Bart are finally reinscribed. Selden unravels the plot and realizes the "self"-sacrifice Lily made by burning the letters.

The final reintegration of the zones/selves comes, then, when "[h]e saw that all the conditions of life had conspired to keep them apart" (317). Lily and Selden finally experience a "fleeting victory over themselves" (317), and as Selden kneels by her deathbed, the selves reunite through a "word which made all clear" (317). In this reading, the cry, "When may I come to you?" is a calling of the fragmented female self to her repressed self, linguistically signified in the letters, the word, and Selden.

The Word is a self-reflective sign that sends us back to a semiotic decoding of the *tableaux vivant* scene. As Candace Waid notes, "Lily spells out letters and herself embodies the sign" (30) in the *tableaux vivant* scene. Selden and Lily clue the reader in on Wharton's semiotic exchange, in which Selden remarks that "there are sign-posts—but one has to know how to read them," to which Lily responds, "Whenever I see you, I find myself spelling out the letter of the sign" (65). This "sign" is tied to the word exchanged between Lily and Selden after her death and connects the *tableaux vivant* scene, the performed marriage of the self with the reclaimed nongendered selves of Lily/Selden. Wharton shares with Woolf a modernist distaste for "[i]mmutably fixed gender identities" as described by Toril Moi (13).

Wharton, it can be argued, experimented with modernist notions of self. Viewing Wharton as a precursor to Woolf adds considerable depth to analysis of her work. The question of the selves of Clarissa Dalloway is a central preoccupation of Woolf's novel, and Woolf freely uses other character zones to articulate the selves of Clarissa in an open-structured form of personality. Clarissa, like Lily Bart, experiences multiple selves, especially in the performing arena of the social event. Even Clarissa herself claims that at a "party she had this feeling of not being herself and that every one was unreal in one way; much more real in another" (171). Clearly Clarissa and Lily Bart suffer from a societal refraction of the self, in which "the body as represented in the text is a site of discourse where social, psychological and spatial conflicts are played out" (Kemp 108).

Clarissa's telling description of her "self" when she "drew the parts together," as she dressed for her party, sets up the culmination of the moment when she integrates her performing disarticulated, fragmented selves. The body (or selves) of Clarissa becomes almost indistinguishable from her linen and china. Lucy calls her ladyship "mistress of silver, of linen, of china" (38). The party itself is described as an important spectacle of surveillance for all the participants, with the hostess prevailing over the entries and announcements of socially important bodies, only to be disrupted by the news of the death of Septimus Warren Smith.

Clarissa's reaction supports a reading of character zones of a symbolic linguistic order in which live "selves" and dead "selves" are mutable and exchangeable: "[I]n the middle of my party, here's death, she thought" (183). Clarissa then begins to experience *jouissance* with the integration of abjection and sexuality. Woolf emphasizes Clarissa's giving in to her repressed body: "He had killed himself—but how? Always her body went through it first, when she was told, suddenly, of an accident, her dress flamed, her body burnt" (184).

Her body sexually awakened, Clarissa begins exploring the borders of her dialogic selves. She experiences the voices around her as impressionist displays underscoring her separation from the performing sphere of the party. She hears Sally ask, "[A]re we not all prisoners?" (192). Clarissa is seemingly rendered speechless by the comment, and the party goers begin speaking about her as if she were not present. "She was like a lily, Sally said, a lily by the side of the pool" (193). Indeed, like Lily Bart, Septimus Warren Smith becomes like a lily or a "death trope," as used by Sandra Kemp, who reminds us, "Death is the moment of supreme identity with our bodies[; it] . . . is the ultimate meditation on solitude—on the possibility of transcending despair" (109). While Whartons's Lily Bart reintegrates her performing selves through death, Virginia Woolf's Clarissa Dalloway achieves a similar result through association with the death of Septimus Warren Smith.

Like *The House of Mirth*, *Mrs. Dalloway* ends with a phrase that sends the reader back into the narrative to a revealing moment that is important as a signifier of the possibility for symbolic reintegration of fragmented selves. Peter Walsh, like Lawrence Selden, has the final word on the central female character. "What is this terror?" [he asks himself, and,] "What is it that fills me with extraordinary excitement? It is Clarissa, he said. For there she was" (194). The phrase "For there she was" is carefully woven into the earlier scene in which Peter tries to convince himself he is not in love with her. However, in denying his abjection and melancholy, he cannot repress her image. "But it was Clarissa one remembered, . . . there she was however; there she was" (76). If Peter is read as a fragmented self, Clarissa has finally reclaimed her body through the reinscription of selves.

If we accept Hélène Cixous's phrase "a feminine text cannot fail to be more than subversive" (888), we can identify Wharton and Woolf as women writers who attacked phallocentric constructs and ideologies. Reading *The House of Mirth* as a premodernist text, and juxtaposing it with *Mrs. Dalloway*, allows for a modernist feminist reading of the text as a subversive experimental female narrative. Lily Bart continues to reclaim her denied selves through our continual readings, just as Clarissa Dalloway causes us to rethink and reform our selves.

Wharton and Woolf created fluid and fragmented performances that are reformed with complex uses of language and dialogisms in their ambiguous female endings. Both novelists articulate the tension between "truth" and "appearance" and illustrate the "innumerable sharp teeth" of the disciplinary social decorum of turn-of-the-century life, yet both novelists share an ability to display the fragmented female self through the use of performing bodies and a feminist modernist dialogism. What is most important, the character zones or open structure identities used by Woolf and Wharton incorporate the Kristevan notion of the chora, a site described by Nancy Armstrong as one in which "the true 'self' is multiple, even duplicitous . . . neither masculine, nor feminine, neither one class nor another, neither unified nor incoherent, but fluid and unconstrained by the categories of any discourse other than its own, including that of psychoanalysis" ("The Rise" 145).

By performing feminist dialogisms, these women novelists confront the symbolic realm of identity and allow the reader to "see the subject not as some entity foreclosed in the structure of language and constituted for once and for all, but as a dynamic and unstable process involving both the imaginary and the symbolic," as one critic asserts of Mrs. Dalloway (Wang 178). *The House of Mirth* and *Mrs. Dalloway* are indeed examples of feminist dialogism designed to disrupt official modes of discourse through an examination of the performing body.

9

Early Women Filmmakers as Social Arbiters: "The Gaze of Correction"

Few are aware that the early days of motion pictures were in many ways the "heydays" of women filmmakers. Before the cinema was recognized as a major form of commerce, and before the role of director became strictly male-defined, women directors were quite common in the early days of cinema from 1896 to the 1920s. Women were not only directors but also writers, producers, and inventors of early motion pictures. Only recently have we begun to understand the contributions of these pioneering women who were largely ignored in early film histories. Ironically, women filmmakers were hugely popular and well known to their contemporaries. They have been omitted from film history for a number of reasons, primarily sexism, but also because of the way sexism has informed the way in which films have been remembered, canonized, and preserved. Janet Staiger, in her essay "The Politics of Film Canons," notes that "[s]elective choices based on criteria supposedly for the good of society end up being canons supportive of the interests of a hegemonic society, not necessarily in the interests of all segments of that culture or all cultures" (196).

The complex politics of film canonization and preservation has led to the destruction and loss of the films of many women directors, African American filmmakers, and many others, whose work questions and problematizes hegemonic society. Though there have been great strides in rediscovery, preservation, and scholarship on early women filmmakers and early African American filmmakers, many stubborn film specialists are unable to recognize and value the work of these filmmakers because their aesthetic opinions have been informed largely by heterosexist, white supremacist, and nonfeminist value systems. For example, the work of many African American filmmakers simply does not "fit" into a system that does not recognize the cultural value of films that often center around themes such as religion, "passing," and other specifically African American cultural values and ideas. "Social message" films are routinely ignored or maligned by film historians. Similarly, women filmmakers' social message, melodramas, and romances have been systematically dismissed by late-twentieth-century critics. Many of these films are now being rediscovered and reevaluated by feminist critics and scholars in African American film. It should be remembered that these works were not oddities outside of an invented and constructed film history. They were viewed and reviewed by contemporary audiences; it was only later that they were seemingly lost to mainstream hegemonic film history and then "added on" as oddities.

Similarly, women and African Americans were central in the construction of the novel, and only now have literary critics begun rewriting the history of the rise of the novel. It is interesting to see the parallels between these reconstruction efforts. Women novelists, like early women filmmakers, were highly popular, and their work was often, though emphatically not always, centered around melodrama, social message, and romance. Similarly, women novelists were systematically excluded from literary canons until scholars began to recognize the cultural value of their work. I do not wish to suggest that early women filmmakers or novelists limited themselves to melodrama, sentiment, social message, or romance; in fact, they wrote in all genres. However, it is clear that sentiment and social message were not highly valued when film or literature canons were being formed. In the same fashion, the central concerns of African American literary and filmic productions were not valued by hegemonic forces. For example, Frances E. W. Harper's novel *Minnie's Sacrifice* was only rediscovered when Frances Smith Foster stumbled upon a chapter of the novel in an issue of the *Christian Recorder,* a newspaper published by the African Methodist Episcopal Church. Earlier scholars had simply not thought to look for literature in African American and Christian popular literature. The excavation of nonhegemonic texts, both film and literary, is only possible because of a widespread reexamination of the canonization process and a questioning of the aesthetics that informed such a process.

The question of aesthetics is directly related to the issues I have raised in this book about power and social discourse. Women filmmakers, both black and white, had a platform essentially on which to tell people how to behave. These social message films have been largely denied entrance into the white male canon because of their female centeredness and their black centeredness. In this chapter, I will discuss the films of women directors and view them as a form of performative conduct texts. I have subtitled the chapter "The Gaze of Correction" to emphasize the role of the "gaze" or the look of the film back at the audience. The filmic gaze refers to the gaze that is behind the camera, like the pen of the author, and the gaze of the film that looks out into the audience and preaches, like the orator. Both gazes wield considerable influence on society and societal behavior. Early women filmmakers, like early African Americans and women orators, use the platform of popular culture to speak publicly, and thus turn around the objectifying gaze of hegemonic authority. These films allowed women to speak and gaze, and yet not be subject to an objectifying gaze.

Quite often, early women's films centered around arranged-marriage themes. Clearly, women filmmakers used film as a platform on which to fight against sexism and the treatment of women as chattel.

In Cleo Madison's *Her Bitter Cup* (1916), an early feminist melodrama, a factory owner forces an impoverished woman into a sexual relationship. In another Cleo Madison film, *Her Defiance* (1916), a young woman who has been seduced, undone, and abandoned is nearly forced by her father into marriage with a wealthy older man. The young woman does the unthinkable. She disrupts the wedding with emphatically defiant gestures and speech. "You fool," she says in a title, as she flees the wedding. Cleo Madison encodes the film with a cleverly placed prop in the wedding scene of an oversized Bible on a table in the middle of the set. Thus, the woman defies not only the word of her father but also the word of the father in the scene. In a scene comparable to that of Eliza's flight in *Uncle Tom's Cabin,* the woman flees in her wedding dress in a stolen stagecoach, finding freedom in the landscape of the woman's text. The film then segues into a romantic narrative in which the woman finds her lover, forgives him, only on her terms, and lives happily ever after. Her defiance "validates the narrative renovation of female space—a space which not only shelters but constructs, then defines, the woman" (Barnes 11).

Cleo Madison's early films are not unique or unprecedented in their feminist melodramatic themes. Another woman filmmaker, Ida May Park, made hundreds of films in the period of the suffragette/New Woman. Unfortunately, all of her films appear to be lost. However, Park's films such as *Bondage* (1917), *The Model's Confession* (1917), and *Risky Road* (1917) center around women who refuse to be victimized by forced sexual relationships or arranged marriages.

Though most of Ida May Park's films are lost, several domestic comedies of filmmaker Alice Guy-Blaché have survived. Guy-Blaché's films of this period also contain female heroines who outwit arranged marriages and other forms of domestic captivity. *His Double* (1913) and *Canned Harmony* (1912) rework almost the same exact plot. Both center around female trickster figures who outwit their father's plans for their arranged marriages. Both pass off their desired suitors as the men their father wishes them to marry by dressing up the men in false disguises until they are married. In *His Double*, for example, the female heroine is going to be forced to marry "Count Laking Coin." Through an elaborate ruse, she disguises her boyfriend as Count Laking Coin and marries him. In *Canned Harmony*, the heroine's father is a music professor, and he wishes her to marry an accomplished musician. She is in love with a man who cannot play an instrument. He dresses up as a violinist, and the heroine plays the Victrola as the impostor pretends to play the violin. The marriage ruse is pulled off, and the couple is found out. Patriarchal ownership of women is questioned in both films. The Law of the father and the Word of the father are called into question by the heroine and Alice Guy-Blaché's gaze of correction.

A House Divided (1913), also directed by Alice Guy-Blaché, explores the freedom of the female body, ownership of place, public speech, and subjectivity. In the cramped set of the American home, a couple has a disagreement and decides not to speak to one another. They agree to communicate through written notes. Here the female heroine uses silence to liberate herself form an unequal domestic arrangement. She holds her husband hostage, in a sense, unable to communicate with her through the spoken word. Interestingly enough, the husband sees a (male) lawyer about the arrangement, seeking patriarchal legitimacy, while the wife seeks advice from a matriarchal figure, presumably her mother. The women laugh at the men, looking through the notes together. The couple reunites when they think there is a burglar in the house. Reunited in a more equal relationship, the husband and wife are almost split up again by the lawyer. However, they ignore him because their marriage is no longer one of inequality. It is regendered in the romantic comedy tradition into a female-centered arrangement of love. In all three of these Alice Guy-Blaché domestic comedies, the film, as conduct text, reenvisions the home as a female center of philosophical freedom.

Women directors consistently used either serious or humorous melodrama to displace female objectification and powerlessness. Seduction and abandonment are played out in films by Dorothy Davenport Reid and Lois Webster. *The Red Kimona*, though actually credited to director Walter Lang, is a Dorothy Davenport Reid production, and Reid is said to have largely directed the film. From an original story by Adela Rogers St. Johns, and a scenario by Dorothy Arzner (who would later become one of the most successful Hollywood women directors), *The Red Kimona* is a feminist exposé about a woman who kills her ex-lover in a moment of passion and falls into a life of prostitution.

The Red Kimona was based on a true story of the life of Gabrielle Darley. Unfortunately, screenwriter Adela Rogers St. Johns neglected to protect Darley's anonymity and even used her name in the film. Darley sued Reid and won. Despite the suit, *The Red Kimona* did very well at the box office. The film stars Priscilla Bonner and is introduced by Dorothy Davenport Reid herself (in a plea for understanding of wayward women). Reid's *Red Kimona* (1925) is another narrative of a pregnant woman who is seduced and abandoned. Instead of accepting her fate, this transgressive heroine murders her ex-lover, and her actions are completely sanctioned by the director's handling of the material. The film has a pronounced use of the female gaze of correction. The first surprise is the use of the opening direct address of the director herself. The device of direct appeal to the reader/viewer is an immediately recognizable feature borrowed from early women's novels. The melodramatic direct appeal promotes audience identification with a transgressive female figure and disrupts the viewer/reader's passive position.

Another important regendering occurs when the heroine kills her ex-lover. The cinematic space of the bound woman becomes radically altered as a space of violent insurrection and justice. Reid sets this scene in a jewelry shop, where the Philistine male figure appears to be buying a ring to ensnare and enslave another woman. The jewels signify the plantocratic tradition of subjugation through manacles and promises. When the heroine shoots him, she not only ends her own captivity, but she insures that no other woman will become his slave. This radical departure from film practice frees the heroine from suffering and guilt. Reid places a signifying cross directly behind the woman in the scene of the killing. Another cross appears on the wall of the jail cell where the woman awaits her sentence. In an amazingly feminist conception, the prison space is depicted as a safe female zone where the heroine is consoled by a sympathetic female prison warden. The transgressive heroine is absolved of guilt by the cross and by the series of glances from the female warden. The jail cell is transformed into a site of slippage between the signifiers of female friendship, female absolution, and male bondage. *The Red Kimona* is often dismissed as being melodramatic and therefore trite, but the film's melodrama provides a platform for a conduct text of considerable importance.

Lois Weber's *Japanese Idyll* (1912) is a conduct narrative of sorts in which a wealthy white merchant purchases a Japanese woman as a mail-order bride. Weber uses tinting to infuse the film with a distinctive moral indignation. In a red-tinted scene, a sinister-looking "wealthy merchant" gazes lecherously at a postcard of Cherry Blossom. He purchases her from an Asian couple involved in the slave trade. The red tint suggests evil incarnate and is underscored by a series of shots of cramped interiors, which involve shady dealings. When Cherry Blossom and her boyfriend discover her fate, the scene is tinted blue to suggest moral good. The couple escapes the sinister marriage merchants into a blue-tinted scene of the outdoors, where they take a boat to freedom. The use of outdoor footage suggests freedom from the marriage of captivity and enslavement.

Escape is the narrative center of scores of films by early serial queens, such as Gene Gauntier, Ruth Stonehouse, Kathlyn Williams, Cleo Madison, and Grace Cunard, who starred and codirected *The Broken Coin* (1915), *The Purple Mask* (1916), *The Mysterious Leopard-Lady* (1914), and *Lady Raffles* (1914). Serial heroines enacted conduct narratives and "signaled the emergence of the New Woman. She wore less restrictive clothes, she was active, she went everywhere she wanted, and she was capable of resolving mysteries, solving problems, and escaping from danger" (Bowser 186). These strong action heroines signify an almost completely forgotten cultural moment in which women were portrayed as active, clever, and physically adroit warrior women who broke from captivity, saved themselves, and even saved others. Grace Cunard's *Purple Mask* featured a female Robin Hood who consistently outwitted the authorities on her trail. Gene Gauntier's early 1908–1909 production of *The Adventures of a Girl Spy* revolved around the adventures of a cross-dressing "girl spy" in an adventure action narrative set in the nineteenth century. Grace Cunard's *Last Man on Earth* (1929) inverted the usual gender configuration. In this film, Cunard plays a gangster who kidnaps and takes captive the last living man on earth and holds him for ransom from an all-woman government. The serial heroines marketed themselves as defiant heroines who reveled in freedom of the body, public speech, freedom of action, and ownership of space in a manner that disappeared from the silver screen until the adventures of *Thelma and Louise* and other action heroines.

As conduct texts, female-centered and female-directed action serials taught women that they could behave freely. These texts, no doubt, exerted a huge influence on the growing popularization of the ideas behind women's rights as well as the movements themselves. Interestingly, women etiquette writers, such as the wildly popular Emily Post, were at the same time exerting a great deal of antifeminist rhetoric. While Emily Post was encouraging women to stay home and perfect the home, women filmmakers were encouraging women in an opposite manner. Similarly, today we are witnessing the rise of the etiquette maven Martha Stewart, who asserts a growing degree of power over women, while at the same time, popular discourse instructs women that they are free from domestication and the domestic space. Then as now, women have been subject to a variety of conflicting messages about how to behave properly.

Linda (1929), directed by Dorothy Davenport Reid, is an exemplification of the conflicting messages that women could expect in popular discourse. Though the film is in many ways a feminist conduct text, it is also, in some ways, a film that espouses traditional values for women.

The central character is in many ways a combination of the nineteenth-century embodiment of the "Angel in the House" and a feminist New Woman.

Perhaps an examination of Reid's life sheds light on the double-voiced-ness of Reid herself. Reid was an embodiment of the New Woman and the Angel of the House. Like the heroine of *Linda*, Reid was viewed as the perfect wife and homemaker. Dorothy Davenport Reid (known as Mrs. Wallace Reid) was born into a well-known family of actors (her parents were Harry and Alice Davenport). At 16, Dorothy herself was an actress. At 18, she married Wallace Reid. They were both successful, especially Wallace Reid. However, Wallace Reid died of a drug overdose in 1923. (He had become addicted to morphine as a result of a car accident.)

Immediately after Wallace Reid's death, Dorothy Davenport Reid began a personal crusade against drug addiction. She starred in *Human Wreckage*, directed by John Griffith Wray, but supervised by Reid herself. It was one of many social message pictures that Reid involved herself in, either as actor, producer, writer, or director. The film is typical of the times in that it is part of a larger development known as the "uplift movement." Women directors and exhibitors found a voice in the uplift movement. Motion pictures were used as vehicles for social good, and women directors such as Lois Weber and Dorothy Reid became a public voice against the evils of drugs, prostitution, poverty, and the abuse of women.

Linda deals with an arranged marriage of sorts. In the film, Linda (Helen Foster) is more or less "sold" in marriage by her father. The arranged marriage theme allowed women directors a melodramatic trope around which to raise the issues of women's place in society and a place to criticize the treatment of women. As we have seen, the arranged marriage trope offered women spectators a highly overwrought narrative of oppression and self-liberation with which they could identify. (This narrative continues to be just as successful with women audiences as we have seen in *Titanic,* a lurid melodrama about an arranged marriage disguised as an action picture.)

Though *Linda* seems to conform to the standard melodramatic form, there are several surprising elements in the film that would suggest a feminist reading. First, though Linda is forced to marry someone easily old enough to be her father or grandfather (Noah Beery Sr.), the role, as played by Beery Sr., is rather sympathetic. Within the narrative, there is a time Linda mistakenly believes that the character played by Beery Sr. is a bigamist, but, oddly, in this film, it is the figure of Linda's father who is an embodiment of an evil force of patriarchy. To some extent, Reid softens her critique of the father here, who himself is a victim of poverty and ignorance. The second factor that is surprising in Linda is the strong message about the need for education and, what is more important, women's education. At one point in the film, Linda picks up and goes to get herself an education, leaving her child with a traveling saleswoman in the interim. In the standard women's melodrama, a central female figure "falls" or is "corrupted," must suffer, and eventually finds redemption.

Linda spends a good deal of the movie *not* suffering, instead being educated, refined, and courted by an attractive young doctor, played by Warner Baxter. Female suffering is limited in this film; the only "suffering" Linda does is to put in time as the wife of an illiterate older man whom she clearly adores as a father figure, rather than a romantic one. Oddly enough, it is the male figure who suffers in *Linda*, when Noah Beery Sr.'s character offers his life for Linda's happiness. *Linda*, like *The Red Kimona*, uses the melodramatic genre to create a transgressive female figure with whom audience members could identify. Both films also promote female friendship as both "fallen women" figures are to a large degree "saved" by other women characters. Linda is aided by a schoolteacher friend, and the central figure of *The Red Kimona* is aided by a female prison warden. *Linda* is a richly rewarding feminist melodrama.

To some extent, Dorothy Davenport Reid herself embodied the spirit of her own melodramatic heroines. In the trades and movie journals, Reid was positioned as a strong heroine in articles such as "Wally's Widow Is Carrying On." She is marketed as a survivor, a friend, and an Angel of the House:

> Dorothy Reid is carrying on the game. Her heart is with the boy whom we all loved so and who lives for her in the person of her small son, Billy. But life has a way of going on, no matter how sorely our hearts are bruised. . . . [Reid is] a woman who has loved deeply and known much sorrow, who has faced issues in her life squarely and courageously. Surely, there can be no room in her soul today for artificiality. . . . Though one of the earliest and finest screen players, you never think of her as an actress, but as a *friend* you can trust. ("Remarkable" 105)

Dorothy Davenport Reid's press image sounds distinctly like that of Oprah Winfrey, herself a powerful female figure who herself has moved into film production, not to mention her work in television advocacy and literacy. Though Reid believed that the primary mission of the screen is to entertain, she also insisted that her films promote the social good. Her voice as a conduct writer was certainly as strong as, if not stronger than, that of Emily Post herself.

The critical reception of Dorothy Davenport Reid was tainted by a strong tendency to dismiss women's melodrama. As Anthony Slide recounts, a *New York Times* critic wrote these vicious remarks about *The Red Kimona*: "There have been a number of wretched pictures in Broadway during the last year, but none seem to have quite reached the low level of *The Red Kimona*, a production evidently intended to cause weep-ing, wailing, and gnashing of teeth" (*Early* 78). The very same elements that audiences adored in melodrama—excess emotion, tragedy, and recovery—were taken to task by critics of the day.

It is interesting that when women directors used elements of excess, melodrama, sensationalism, and moralism, they were (and are) taken to task, but when D. W. Griffith or James Cameron uses these same elements, they are largely celebrated by society. *The Red Kimona* and *Linda* are fine examples of the "women's picture" in that they are constructed by and for women and open up a space to critique gender and class roles. Reid exposed child neglect in *Broken Laws* (1924), confidence schemes in *Sucker Money* (1933), and a young woman's moral downfall in *The Woman Condemned* (1934) and *The Road to Ruin* (1934). She eventually moved out of the motion picture business, noting that "men resent women in top executive positions in film as in any field of endeavor" (*Slide, Early* 78). She continued to write until she retired in 1968, and she died in 1977 at the age of 81.

A stunning print of *Linda* was recovered and restored and is in the collection of the Donnell Library in New York. Efforts to recover more films directed by Reid and other women directors are being made by the Women Film Pioneer Group. As I wrote in 1995, however, "A reexamination of the 'melodramatic,' 'sensationalist,' 'moralist' cinema of Dorothy Davenport Reid and other women directors is long overdue" (*Women* 316).

The films of Lois Weber best exemplify the melodramatic films of her era. Film critics and new historians have begun questioning earlier film criticism that wrote her off as a didactic moralizer. Born in Allegheny, Pennsylvania, Lois Weber was born into an overly devout family. She sang as a Christian Home Missionary, and, after a stint at acting, she began making what she called "missionary pictures" with her husband, Phillips Smalley, in the early 1900s. Anthony Slide notes: "The truth is that few men, before or since, have retained such absolute control over the films they have directed—and certainly no women directors have achieved the all-embracing, powerful status once held by Lois Weber" (*Lois Weber* 6). Weber wrote her own screenplays; produced, edited, and shot her own films; ran her own studio; and was one of the highest paid directors of her time. Her best known film, *The Blot* (1921), is certainly a conduct text, one that preaches against classist behavior and argues that we should pay college professors as much as we pay common laborers. A masterpiece that combines realism and moralist fervor, *The Blot* centers around the story of two families living side by side, one wealthy, and one desperately poor.

The Griggs family is destitute because the father is a college professor who makes very little money. The Olsens, who are much better off, have little or no compassion for their neighbors. In one scene, Mrs. Griggs, driven by a need to take care of her family, steals a chicken from the house of the Olsens. She returns the bird, in the realization of what she has done. When a suitor, Phil West, courts the young Amelia Griggs, he brings a basket of food and a chicken. In a typically melodramatic situation, Amelia believes that her mother stole the Olsens' chicken. Amelia begs for her mother's forgiveness, and Mrs. Olsen is finally moved by Amelia's behavior. Weber's moralism and social statements are beautifully rendered. Her gaze of correction shows us the well-worn shoes of the Griggs family, the torn sofa, and their meager living situation. *The Blot* is a rejection of the values of capitalist America that measures the value of people in wealth and property, and it is thus a deeply feminist film. Much of the narrative is concerned with the future of the young woman Amelia. Will she marry the young suitor, Phil West, who is a student? Will she end up destitute and poverty stricken, like her mother? Or will she marry the Olsen boy? Lois Weber constructs an ending that seems to undercut itself. Amelia marries Phil West, presumably for social mobility, but she obviously still has feelings for another young man. The film's ending can be interpreted in several ways, but perhaps the best way is to see that Weber is making a commentary on what women in certain socioeconomic conditions are forced to do, to marry as soon as possible in order to survive.

In addition to *The Blot*, Lois Weber attacked social hypocrisy in *Hypocrites* (1914) and the plight of women in *What Do Men Want?* (1921). She explored racism and anti-Semitism in *The Jews' Christmas*. In *The People vs. John Doe*, Weber made an anti–capital punishment film. *Hop, the Devil's Brew* (1915) was her contribution to the temperance movement. *Where Are My children?* (1916) argues against abortion and for birth control. Weber found herself at the center of a controversy with the release of *The Hand That Rocks the Cradle* (1917) (subtitled *Is a Woman a Person?*). The film is loosely based on Margaret Sanger's writings that advocated birth control, and Sanger and Emma Goldman were arrested for arguing against a ban of the film. Weber herself played the wife of a physician who would not dispense advice on birth control to his female patients. Weber's character feels compelled to disregard her husband's orders: she gives the women advice on birth control herself and finds herself arrested. The film was censored, but it was finally released. Predictably, it received rather negative reviews. As Kay Sloan recounts, one critic wrote, "The family photoplay theatre . . . is not the proper place for [*The Hand That Rocks the Cradle*]" (342). Many critics deemed the film "propaganda." As a propagandistic conduct text, the film was certainly a success. Lois Weber was not without a sense of humor, however. Her short comic film, *How Men Propose* (1913), is a witty social critique of the marriage proposal that has a decidedly feminist edge. In the film, a woman is proposed to by three men. Each asks her hand in marriage and gives her a ring. The woman plays directly to the audience, gesturing to the camera to show us each ring with delight. The woman gives each of the men a photograph of herself. She tells them to come to her room for her reply. They run into one another and inevitably begin bragging about their engagement, as if she were a piece of property. When they show one another the photograph of the same woman, they know they have been duped. In an unpredictable reversal of gendered behavior, the three men faint from surprise. The men go to her home, seeking an answer for her behavior. There, she has left them each an identical letter:

Dear Friend:
I am returning your ring. I was only playing. I am writing an article on how men propose and wanted some actual experience. You may keep the photo.
Sincerely,
Grace Darling.

The feminist humor in the film is highlighted by the fact that the filmmaker, like Grace Darling, has had the audacity to "play with" such a serious endeavor as the marriage proposal. Much of the humor is in the serial repetition of the gestures of all-consuming passion and ardor made by each successive suitor. In this way, Weber mocks bourgeois American culture and its gestures, as well as the institution of romance itself. A woman character who is writing about what she "should" be pining about is a uniquely transgressive character and a recognizably feminist invention. The film spoofs conduct literature itself in the title, *How Men Propose*. *How Men Propose* is an exciting rediscovery of early feminist cinema in that it demonstrates the humorous side of Lois Weber, pioneer of the conduct film and premier social arbiter of her times.

Apparently, few cultural historians are aware that writer and folklorist Zora Neale Hurston was also a filmmaker. She asserted a black female gaze in a series of untitled ethnographic films that she directed in the early years of the cinema. Fatimah Tobing Rony suggests that Hurston "worked to create her own fieldwork methodology" (205) and that her films were not merely ethnographic spectacles that objectified her subject. Hurston, who "was one of the first African Americans to receive a B.A. from Barnard College" (Rony 203) went to the American South at the urging of Franz Boas, chair of the anthropology department at Barnard during that time. From 1928 to 1929, Hurston made a series of documentary films recording "children's games, dancing, a baptism, and activities in a logging camp, and in 1940 of activities in Beaufort, South Carolina, including road scenes, dock scenes, landscape, the activities of farm workers, prison laborers, and most importantly, the activities of the Commandment Keeper Church, a local African-American church" (Rony 203).

From this work, Hurston learned the need of observation of the various phenomena and people she recorded as if they were separate from her, yet simultaneously a part of the fabric of African American culture. Hurston's films are the work of a gifted amateur, yet also of a budding ethnographer who sought to impose the gaze of the documentarist's camera upon her subject. Hurston would focus on specific actions, according to Rony, breaking her subjects into "types," who would hold "up slips of paper with their ages, filing past the camera frontally and then in profile" (204). Yet, as Rony notes, instances of this rigid "typing" occur when a young woman walks straight toward the camera, staring at the lens, and then offers her right and left profile for inspection, all the time smiling. But after this "parade inspection" pose, Hurston's camera breaks off into what Rony describes as "shots [of] an experimental quality, the camera cutting from a shot of two women on a porch, to an extreme long shot of the garden with the houses in the background, followed by a shot of the young woman lying odalisque-style facing the camera on the porch, concluding with a low-angle shot of a woman's feet rocking on the porch next to the paws of a cat" (204–5).

This elegiac and evocative footage, preserved in the Library of Congress, shows that far from being a relentlessly "objective" observer of that which her lens perceives, Hurston can break through the rigid role of the ethnographer to become an interpreter of the world she documents. As Rony notes, Elaine Charnov has compared this sequence to the languidly sensuous films of Maya Deren, who created a dream world of the everyday in her well-known experimental films of the 1940s. In this sequence, and in the rest of her footage from 1928 through 1929 and 1940, Zora Neale Hurston takes up the challenge of viewing African American life in the American South during the early years of the cinematographic apparatus from a "non-Othered" perspective, using what Hurston termed "the spy-glass of Anthropology" (qtd. in Rony 204) to create a world of visual self-actualization and self-expression rather than a catalogue of externalized stereotypes, no matter how Hurston sought to classify or categorize her subjects in her documentary footage.

As Rony notes, this "'Spy glass' . . . had been traditionally reserved for the white anthropologist, the white scholar who believed in the objective, descriptive recording of so-called 'vanishing' peoples" (204). Of course, the stance of objectivity is itself a construct, miming the detached gaze of the clinical, disinterested viewer as he surveys the subject(s). Zora Neal Hurston instinctively knew, I would argue, that this much sought after stance of objective "fieldwork methodology" (Rony 205) is, in itself, a construct, and that, as she discovered in her documentary filming, the subjects of any ethnographic/cinematic inquiry will always resist being put into roles or categories and continually spill out past the boundaries of the frame into the collective realm of the viewer's visual consciousness.

In a sense, Zora Neale Hurston's footage, for all its insistence on classification and distance, becomes an invaluable document because, as Rony suggests: "What makes [the Commandment Keeper Church footage shot by Hurston in April–May 1940] unlike any other ethnographic research film of its kind is that Hurston herself appears [in the footage] as a participating worshipper, either playing music or walking among the congregation" (207). With this simple yet transcendent act, Hurston appropriates her own presence and physical existence and makes it a part of the spectacle she witnesses, erasing (to a large extent) the traditional boundary between a conventional cinematic ethnographer and her subjects. In these images, Hurston becomes one with the world she observes, entering into the action within the frame, refusing to be exiled to the supposed "safety zone" of absence that marks the domain of the practicing cinematographer. Thus, Hurston's gaze, as an African American documenting the lives and customs of other African Americans, becomes a vision of extraordinary power and intimacy, affording the viewer a degree of proximity to the subject missing in the conventional documentary work of Flaherty, Grierson, and even Maya Deren, in her late Haitian voodoo footage. Zora Neale Hurston steps into the world that she seeks to record and thus acknowledges that she is a part of it, of the shared world of African American culture in the United States in the first half of the twentieth century.

In all of the films discussed in this chapter, then, we have seen the feminist gaze of self-actualization present itself in direct opposition to the patriarchal phallocentric gaze of Griffith, Chaplin, Grierson, Flaherty, and other male cinematic pioneers, in that the films of Alice Guy-Blaché, Lois Weber, Dorothy Davenport Reid, Zora Neale Hurston, and other feminist cinematic pioneers subvert and question the camera's gaze as it had been employed by the dominant male cinema of the period. Guy-Blaché, Weber, Reid, and others set about to create a world in which the feminist gaze supplants the "othering" look of patriarchal narrative cinema and thus give birth to a zone in which their subjects could, in Alice Guy-Blaché's oft-quoted admonition, "Be Natural." Freed from the constraints self-imposed by Edwin S. Porter, W. K. L. Dickson, George Méliès, and others, these feminist cinéastes created a zone of observation and instruction in which one's conduct, actions, beliefs, and practices were opened up to the viewer on a more natural, relaxed level, without many of the inherently othering tactics employed by their male colleagues. The legacy of these feminist cinema pioneers is thus to create a new vision, wholly without precedent, in the emerging art form of the cinema, and thus actualize a zone of self-expression in which the feminist documentarists and narrative filmmakers of the late cinema and early video age could follow.

10

Kasi Lemmons's *Eve's Bayou* as Conduct Text

*E*ve's Bayou (1997), directed by Kasi Lemmons, is but one example of a number of "social message" films made by and for African Americans. African Americans have used a variety of popular culture forms to teach and advocate values and morals, from music to the pulpit; from blues and spirituals to motion pictures; from slave narratives to fiction, poetry, and prose. Though I have located a few black etiquette and conduct texts, including *The Negro in Etiquette: A Novelty* (1899) and *How to Get Along with Black People* (1971), and various poems, including Frances E. W. Harper's "Advice to Girls," I am of the opinion that African Americans rely less on the formal genres of etiquette and conduct texts and more on the Bible, the Koran, and oral tales of instruction for behavioral guidance. African Americans also created forms of popular culture that instruct and guide, including blues, jazz, and motion pictures.

Women blues singers, for example, spoke out against infidelity in songs such as "I Don't Care Where You Take It," sung by Bertha Idaho:

> So I don't care where you take it,
> sweet papa, just move it on out of here,
> Cause this ain't no filling station,
> or no parking place,
> So, I don't care where you take it, sweet papa,
> just move it on out of here.

> (Harrison 103)

In the 1930s, African American filmmaker and preacher Eloyce Gist recreated the film genre of the social message picture into a type of film that specifically instructs and espouses basic Christian principles. With her husband, James Gist, this pioneering evangelist filmmaker created, for one example, a film entitled *Hell Bound Train,* which featured a number of different train cars, each of which carried passengers who had fallen under the sway of a specific and distinct sin. The story line developed along the lines of the outcome of the sinner's behavior. The Gists did not allow the film to be projected without their presence. The film was part of a traveling religious program that included preaching by both Eloyce and James Gist. The program was supplemented with hymns and spirituals. This unusual handling of film projection and manipulation of spectatorship recreates the moving picture into a type of oval storytelling/preaching method common to African American culture. The Gists' films were rediscovered by film historians Thomas Cripps and Gloria Hudson; however, they still await restoration by the Library of Congress. This distinctly unique and African American genre of film should be recognized as a form of the conduct text. Though few are familiar with the early films of African American women, such as Eloyce Gist, Zora Neale Hurston, Eslanda Goode Robeson and Alice B. Russell, because of film availability, many African American film scholars are familiar with the films of pioneering black male filmmakers, such as Spencer Williams and Oscar Micheaux. A fine exemplification of the conduct films of Oscar Micheaux is *Swing* (1938), in which a seamstress tries to stop her husband from gambling and philandering. In *The Symbol of the Unconquered* (1920), also directed by Oscar Micheaux, an African American heiress fights off the Ku Klux Klan to save her land. Similarly, in Spencer Williams's *The Blood of Jesus*, an African American woman faces the choice between religious salvation and hell.

With the resurgence of the new independent African American cinema, African American directors such as the Hudson brothers, Julie Dash, Leslie Harris, George Tillmann Jr., and Kasi Lemmons are reinventing a form of conduct cinema for modern audiences. *Tales from the Hood* (1995), directed by Rusty Cundieff, appropriates the form of the British omnibus horror film *Dead of Night* (1945) and renarrates the four story segments within the film from an Afrocentric perspective. In an era in which preaching and social message pictures themselves are critically devalued, *Tales from the Hood* combines entertainment with social messages specifically targeted toward African Americans. The film is anti-drug, promotes the value of friendship and comradeship, and teaches its audience how to survive white supremacist culture at large. In a series of densely structured vignettes, Clarence Williams, as Mr. Simms, ostensibly the owner of a neighborhood funeral parlor, narrates a series of cautionary tales for several young gang members, stressing the need for family solidarity, living a "clean and sober" existence, and staying out of trouble with the authorities. At the film's end, however, Mr. Simms is revealed to be Satan himself, and the young gang members he lectured see themselves in coffins, victims of random drug and gang violence. As one of a number of commercially successful new films from African American directors, *Tales from the Hood* seeks both to entertain and to instruct its audience.

Just Another Girl on the I.R.T. (1993, Leslie Harris) teaches how to handle teen pregnancy and how to survive a Brooklyn housing project and make it to medical school. Julie Dash's *Daughters of the Dust* (1991) also may be viewed as a conduct text. The filmmaker strongly conveys the importance of maintaining and understanding African American familial ties in this saga about the Gullah, descendants of slaves who settled in South Carolina and Georgia.

Eve's Bayou has much in common with *Daughters of the Dust,* in that it also stresses the importance of keeping an oral history of the family, in this case the fictional family of Eve Batiste. *Eve's Bayou*, like *Daughters of the Dust*, centers around a place and its peoples. Eve's Bayou is a fictional place named after Eve Batiste, who, legend has it, used alternative medicine to save the life of Jean Claude Batiste, a white man who later freed Eve for her generosity and gave her the piece of land that has become known as "Eve's Bayou." The film is narrated and told from the point of view of a descendent of Eve, a young girl also named Eve, and it is itself a conduct text that preaches the value of family history and memory; the importance of family ties and self-respect; and a respect for marriage, voodoo, and elders.

Briefly, the main plot of the film centers around Eve, who believes she killed her father by using voodoo because she was angry at him for his continual philandering and for possibly sexually abusing Eve's sister, Cicely. But because the film is told through a child's eyes, as she grows into understanding, we also grow into seeing the complexity of the story. It is a rather complicated *bildungsroman,* as well as an African American conduct text. From a cinematic point of view, *Eve's Bayou* is notable for its narrative structure, which includes multiple points of view, multiple perspectives, and a blending of diegetic space and time that is achieved by a unique narratorial strategy. In scenes that are reminiscent of early African American films, which often incorporate flashbacks and memory sequences with the use of mattes, *Eve's Bayou* often cuts to flashbacks and memory sequences. In early African American cinema, a character might be telling a story, for example, about something in the past, and part of the frame might include a matte painting that represents the story visually. In some cases, these matte paintings would interact with the onscreen action; for example, ghosts, spirits, and apparitions interact with the actors in several early African American films. This blurs diegetic (onscreen) space and time configurations, in that diegetic time and space are seemingly in contact with extradiegetic (offscreen) time and space. In *Eve's Bayou*, Kasi Lemmons reworks this traditional blending of diegetic and extradiegetic time and space in a manner that is both a homage to early African American filmmakers and an appropriation of French avant garde memory-editing techniques, popularized by such filmmakers as Marguerite Duras, Alain Resnais, and Alain Robbe-Grillet. In *Eve's Bayou*, as in films of the memory-editing school and early African American films, characters interact across and among diegetic and extradiegetic space. For example, Mozelle Batiste, Eve's aunt, who is a spiritual medium, is able to tell her stories (and thus instruct Eve) in a number of remarkable sequences that transcend diegetic screen time and space. In these sequences, we watch as Mozelle tells her stories and they come alive, not through traditional flashbacks, but within the frame (and diegetic space) in which she tells the story. As she tells the story of the loss of the three men in her life, for example, Mozelle looks in a mirror, and outside of the mirror, the three men appear.

It is clear that Eve shares Mozelle's ability to act as a medium. She is frightened by her ability to foretell the future through visions, and she is also able to see other people's memories, and experience them, by touching their hands. Nevertheless, she is not infallible, and part of her coming of age is learning that she can be manipulated or just plain wrong in her interpretation of events. In an early scene in the film, Eve (Jurnee Smollett) is awakened by the sound of lovemaking. She is shocked to see her father, Louis (Samuel L. Jackson), making love with Matty Mereaux. After she tells her sister what happened, her sister, Cicely (Meagan Good), trying to shield their mother from their father's infidelities, manipulates Eve into thinking that what she saw was not infidelity but something more innocent. In a shared flashback of sorts, Cicely reconstructs Eve's memory. Cutting across diegetic and extradiegetic space and time configurations, the girls are seen in the carriage house where Eve witnessed her father's infidelity. The girls watch as Cicely reconstructs a shared memory. We hear Cicely narrate in a voice-over, "Daddy told her a joke, and she fell on him laughing," as we see this innocent interpretation of events. Suddenly, we are back in the little girls' bedroom, where Eve, not sure what to believe, is reassured by Cicely. This scene has the effect of teaching the audience the power of memory, which is the main theme of the film. At the beginning of *Eve's Bayou*, we hear the phrase, "Memory is a selection of images. Some elusive, others printed indelibly on the brain." At the end of the film, we hear this same refrain, but we also learn that "the truth changes color, depending to the light. . . . Each image is like a thread. Each thread, woven together to make a tapestry of intricate texture, and the tapestry tells a story, and the story is our past."

Eve learns the importance of understanding the complexity of shared memories, and she learns that even though she is "gifted with sight," her tales are part of a complex interwoven oral history of the Batiste family and of African American history in the broad sense. The viewer shares the experience of Eve and is invited to learn the value and complexity of history and memory. Though *Eve's Bayou* can be read as a conduct text, it is never simple, preachy, or linear; instead, viewers are left to interpret the material and narratives in keeping with their own experiences. Thus, few would agree about what exactly happens in the Batiste family. In some ways, the emphasis on the fallibility of memory makes viewing the film as a conduct text a bit problematic. In addition to the question of the validity of memory, *Eve's Bayou* is also lacking in stereotypical and binary "Good" and "Evil" characterizations. Louis Batiste, played by Samuel L. Jackson, is a fully developed character who is capable of both good and evil actions. He is the town doctor, and he is obviously a philanderer of outrageous proportions. There is no doubt that he hurts his wife, Roz (played by Lynne Whitfield), terribly by his infidelities. But there is also no doubt that he loves his family deeply, and he himself is pained by his own evils. He is also punished in the narrative: he is murdered by the husband of Matty Mereaux (Lisa Nicole Carson), with whom he had been having an affair, and he leaves a letter that attempts to explain his infidelity as a weakness and a character flaw: "I'm just a small town doctor pushing aspirin to the elderly. But to a certain type of woman I'm a hero. I need to be a hero sometimes." When Eve reads her father's letter, she learns to accept him as a human being with a deep character flaw. Like Eve, we as the audience learn the power of healing through understanding and forgiving. The letter also solves the more thorny issue of whether or not Louis sexually molested his daughter Cicely. Like Eve, we, as audience members, assume the worst is true, and like Eve, we want him to die. But we learn from the letter that Louis, in a drunken stupor, mistook his daughter for his wife, kissed her sexually, and slapped her out of anger at himself, when he realized what he was doing. Louis's version of events is only one memory, and it is problematized by Cicely's memories of the event, as well as our tendency to vilify Louis because we know him already to be an adulterer. Kasi Lemmons refuses to carve out the "truth" for us in black and white. She beautifully captures the nebulous and transient reality characteristic of many mythic events and family stories.

That Lemmons is able to render such a highly charged issue as incest and avoid its stereotypical handling is a remarkable feat. Within the frame, she cuts across diegetic space, but as viewers, we are left to reflect on the resonances that are refracted like light onto our own family narratives, which so often force us into a position of choosing whom to believe. In cases of sexual abuse, we have been taught to always believe the child, but in some cases, it is possible that there has been a misunderstanding. *Eve's Bayou* reminds us not to be too quick in our judgments and to hear all sides of a story; indeed, it reminds us that there are always many different memories of the same event. Cicely's memory of the event is not incorrect, the film suggests, but merely informed by a young woman's point of view. From her perspective, she was molested. Louis is certainly not completely exonerated for his behavior. His drunkenness is no excuse for kissing his daughter like a woman, nor is his character flaw an excuse for his extramarital affair. In the larger context of the film, as conduct text, the message is clear: Louis's behavior is unacceptable, and he is riding for a fall. His death is no surprise, and the message is clear: This behavior will make you lose your family and lose your life.

While *Eve's Bayou* questions the fallibility of memory, it champions the value of voodoo and prophesy within the African American community. Through Eve's eyes, we learn the tale of Eve's Aunt Mozelle, a spiritualist who is disregarded by Louis as a "crazy" person but who is respected and revered by Fran Mére (Ethyl Ayler), who reminds Louis that "in my day—we were happy for signs and warnings." Kasi Lemmons's handling of voodoo and spirituality in *Eve's Bayou* reflects the African American cultural acceptance of Pan-African spirituality. Eve is taught to respect her gift for precognition and to be careful not to invoke voodoo unless she is absolutely sure she means it. In short, the power of vision itself is one of the main themes of the film.

The opening montage of *Eve's Bayou* includes a blurry black and white series of images, presumably one of Eve's visions or perhaps a glimpse inside the memory of the narrator herself. At the end of the montage, the director cuts to a close-up of Eve's eyes and then to an extreme close-up of one of Eve's eyes. The film dissolves into the iris where we begin to see a series of tracking pans across the bayou. We see images of overhanging moss and the magisterial vistas of the water and land of the South. Not only is this vision Eve's point of view, but it is her very subjectivity: we are invited to share her subjectivity, her alterity, and witness and experience her coming of age as visionary. This extraordinary manipulation of the experience of the viewer denies the viewer the traditional role of passive voyeur. It is as if the film itself is a ritual passage of experience and knowledge, and we share in Eve's struggle to come to grips with her past and present. At the beginning of the film, Eve's unraveled memory hints at the possibility of sexual abuse of Cicely, and Eve's voice-over narration strongly suggests that she believes she killed her father: "The summer I killed my father, I was ten years old. My brother Poe was nine, and my sister Cicely had just turned fourteen." The narrator repeats this phrase, at the end of the film, but with a slight difference: "The summer my father said goodnight, I was ten years old. My brother Poe was nine, and my sister had just turned fourteen." The narrator and the viewer experience the passage of experience that teaches and instructs us how to interpret Eve's visions and experiences. Like Eve, we must begin to "learn to see," in a relearning process. Eve, a young girl, is subject to frightening visions.

Eve's first vision, or premonition, occurs when her Uncle Harry (played by Branford Marsalis) is killed in a car accident after leaving a party drunk— far too drunk to drive. In a black and white montage sequence reminiscent of *Persona*, we see a pendulum, Harry, a grave, and several other images in rapid succession. The montage ends with a shot of Harry saying goodnight to Eve, calling her "Red," her nickname.

Eve is seemingly unaware of her own abilities in terms of precognition. She is a child, and she is neither frightened nor surprised by her supernatural gift. She is sexually unaware, a carefree spirit who behaves much like a trickster, teasing her brother with chocolate-covered bees and teasing her older sister when she gets her first period. Eve seeks to understand the sexual and the supernatural. She follows her father around while he "tends" to his patients, and she spends a great deal of time eavesdropping on her Aunt Mozelle, who gives psychic readings in her home. She develops a special and strong relationship with Mozelle, and she learns many lessons from life story.

Mozelle thinks of herself as a tragic black widow. Ironically, she admits to Eve, she can see others' futures, but not her own. Mozelle sets an example for Eve of someone who recognizes her limitations and uses her gift responsibly. When a woman comes to hear her future from Mozelle, she begs to be told of the whereabouts of her son. Mozelle "sees" a black and white flash of images of a young man shooting dope. She tells the woman that she will be able to find her son in the hospital, that he is a junkie. She helps others with her gift, and yet she is aware that she herself has a blind spot. She is unable to move forward in her life because of her past. If *Eve's Bayou* is a *bildungsroman,* it is also a multiple coming of age story. Mozelle not only acts as an instructor and guide to Eve, but she also undergoes a complete change by the end of the film.

Early in the film, Mozelle and Roz, her sister-in-law, visit a psychic, Elzora (played by Diahann Carroll). Elzora tells Mozelle that she is a curse, a black widow, and that the next man she marries will die. Elzora reinforces Mozelle's self-doubt and fears. She is motivated by professional jealousy, perhaps, or meanness. Elzora does, however, intuit that Roz is in pain. She predicts that there will be an end to Roz's problems. Roz is at this time under enormous stress because she's aware that her husband, Louis, is having extramarital affairs. Elzora tells her to look to her children, and when Mozelle has a premonition of a bus accident, Roz becomes convinced that one of her children will be killed by a bus in the near future. In a humorous treatment of spiritual beliefs, Roz keeps her children inside for an entire summer because she is convinced that they are in danger. When another child is killed by a bus, the family celebrates and finally goes outside.

Elzora's prophesy is fraudulent in comparison with that of Eve and Mozelle. Elzora is an interesting construct on which the film places the question of the reliability (and responsibility) towards spiritual psychic ability. She is introduced in "white face," in pancake makeup, a mercenary figure who is dismissed by the more knowledgeable Mozelle. She lets Eve think that she has used voodoo against her father, through her own powers, while nodding and winking at the audience. Nevertheless, some of her prophecies seem to come true. She is wrong about Mozelle, who turns her life around; however she was correct when she told Roz "sometimes a soldier falls on his own sword. In three years you will be happy again." It is up to the audience to decide if Elzora is a fraud, but her prophecy seems to come true when Louis is murdered by the husband of the woman he has been adulterating, and Roz is finally happy again, in three years time, after the loss of her husband, Louis. Vision and visionaries are not always what they seem to be in *Eve's Bayou*. The authenticity of Elzora may be hard to ascertain; however Elzora acts as a force not unlike that in a conduct novel, because she teaches Eve to beware of the power of wishing someone dead. Oddly, Eve may not be responsible for her father's death because of her use of voodoo, but because she is indirectly responsible for the events that lead up to her father's death. On her way to see Elzora, Eve meets Lenny Mereaux and strongly insinuates that her father and Lenny's wife are having an affair. In rage, Lenny tracks down Louis in a bar, and after confronting him, he shoots him down. Eve and the audience are left to judge whether or not she is responsible for her father's death, either because she tried to use voodoo against him, or because she unwittingly drove Lenny into a jealous, murderous rage against her father. But ultimately, as the end of the film suggests, Eve comes to understanding and knowledge and remembers the night, not as the "night I murdered my father," but the "night my father said goodnight." Eve understands the complexity of events. Her father is responsible for his own actions, which led to his death.

As a viewer, we participate in the coming-of-age of Eve and Mozelle. Eve makes her father and mother increasingly uncomfortable when she discovers sexuality. For example, she begins back-talking her mother with insinuations about her father's sexual misconduct. Repeating her father's phrase, she says to her mother "there's some illnesses you just can't put a finger on," and later, when she becomes more bold and angry she blurts out that she knows her daddy is not working on "housecalls" on Sunday. But Eve's growing understanding of adult sexuality is not only negative and tinged with adultery and incest. She learns of the power and poetry of sexuality through her growing understanding of Mozelle.

It is through Mozelle that Eve first hears something positive about sexuality. Mozelle carefully explains how she loved all of her three lost husbands differently. She tells of being awakened by a powerful passion by Josiah, for example, and in one of the most powerful scenes in the film, she invites Eve into a vision of what happened when Josiah threatened to break up her marriage with Maynard.

In a striking example of the blending of diegetic and extradiegetic time and space, Mozelle and Eve seem to be "in" the murder scene as she describes it in a voice-over. Mozelle turns to the next room, where the events she describes seem to "come to life." She had been cheating on her husband, Maynard, and she didn't realize how much he loved her until this event, tragically, revealed his love. As Mozelle describes the events, Josiah comes to the house, ready to take Mozelle with him. Maynard intervenes and Josiah pulls a gun on him. Maynard walks up and places his abdomen directly against the gun, saying, "You'll have to kill me, 'cause my wife ain't goin' nowhere."

"In that moment I knew that I loved Maynard," says Mozelle, teaching Eve, and the audience much about the complexity of marriage, sexuality, and adultery. Josiah murders Maynard and flees, and Mozelle is left believing she is a black widow figure. Later, a man named Julian Grayraven (played by Vonde Curtis Hall) falls in love with Mozelle. He wishes to marry her, but she tells him he cannot because she fears he will die as a result. The romance between the two is handled with subtlety and adds to the *bildungsroman* nature of the story. In a very romantic scene, Julian paints Mozelle's portrait as the song "I Want a Sunday Kind of Love" is heard on the Victrola. Eve is privy to this growing relationship, and she learns much from it.

In addition to teaching Eve about spirituality and sexuality, Mozelle offers Eve (and the audience) life lessons, in the form of a highly memorable speech about the metaphysical nature of pain. Her ability to "see" through life goes beyond the level of merely being a vector of sight. Her wisdom has come through life experience. In talking about losing loved ones, Mozelle says, "Life is a series of good-byes. They all hurt terribly. . . . All I know is most people's lives are a great disappointment to them and no one leaves this earth without feeling terrible pain and if there is no divine explanation at the end of it all . . . that's sad." It is no surprise that Debbie Morgan, who plays Mozelle, won the Independent Spirit Award for Best Supporting Female Actor for her performance. Her delivery of the above speech is stunning. She instructs us as much as she does herself and Eve. Mozelle and Eve reconstruct the fall of Eve and the tree of knowledge from a black womanist perspective. Eve is not doomed by her "Fall" from grace. She learns from it. Mozelle is not cursed eternally for eating the forbidden fruit of carnality. Instead, both are offered salvation through self-knowledge gained by vision and self-acceptance and a deeper understanding of spirituality and "vision" itself.

After Louis's death, Mozelle is released by a dream from her belief that she is a black widow. Actually, it is her interpretation of the dream that releases her. She describes the dream to Eve, thus teaching her to learn how to grow up emotionally. In the dream, Mozelle sees herself swimming in air, flying. She sees another woman, another form of herself, frowning midair. She allows that self to drown, wakes up, and agrees to marry Julian. She tells Eve that she has a message from her father, a message of love and forgiveness.

Eve's Bayou is an extraordinary example of a conduct tale. It combines multiple perspectives and multiple tale tellers to culminate in a film that deals with issues as complex as family secrets to incest, prophecy, extramarital affairs, and voodoo. Kasi Lemmons is an extraordinarily gifted visionary. Her film, a study of vision itself, is a reminder that popular films can be entertaining as well as socially redeeming.

But *Eve's Bayou* is not alone as a fine exemplification of the new African American cinema that combines entertainment with essentially a conduct text. *Soul Food* (1997), directed by George Tillman Jr. is another fine example of the genre. In *Soul Food,* an African American family falls apart when the strong grandmother figure is stricken with illness. Her daughters, played by Vanessa Williams, Viveca Fox, and Nia Long are left to fend for themselves. In many ways, they have been shielded from the world and need to learn the lesson that family is the most important and sacred tradition in the African American experience. Like *Eve's Bayou,* *Soul Food* is told through the narration of a child, in this case a young boy who sees his family falling apart around him. He has a strong bond with Big Mamma, the grandmother, and he literally saves the day when the sisters are about to sell his grandmother's house. This house is the site of the great family Sunday dinners. As the film explains, in African American families, the Sunday dinner is almost a sacred time because in slavery, as the film maintains, African Americans had little to celebrate, yet they began the tradition of the huge Sunday dinner. *Soul Food* is in many ways a much more straightforward conduct text than *Eve's Bayou.* It teaches the young boy to stay away from guns, not involve himself in extramarital affairs, and value family. In a rather unbelievable finale, the young boy gathers together the family by promising them a piece of the grandmother's long-lost savings. No such savings exists, as far as the child knows, but unbeknownst to him, in a rather sweet turn of events, it turns out that there is a suitcase full of money.

It is interesting to compare *Soul Food* and *Eve's Bayou* as conduct texts and social message films. In terms of their narrative styles, they could not be more different. *Eve's Bayou* is sophisticated in its narratorial style, unpredictable, and told from a female perspective. *Soul Food* is a much more commercially acceptable, straightforward narrative film, punctuated with the upbeat music of executive producer Kenneth "Babyface" Edmonds. The film is narrated by a young boy and thus more easily marketed to a young male audience, which, of course, dominates the film market economy. *Soul Food* was better distributed, received wider release, and thus fared better in the market place than *Eve's Bayou*. Nevertheless, *Eve's Bayou* is doing very well as a video release partly because of positive word of mouth within the African American community and the art-house circuit crowd.

Not only are both *Eve's Bayou* and *Soul Food* indicative of the revival in contemporary black cinema practice within the dominant cinema, but they also gesture back to the work of Eloyce Gist, Oscar Micheaux, Spencer Williams, and other pioneering African American cinema artists who sought to use the medium of the cinema as a means of both self-expression and instruction. Incorporating a variety of social codings and fabulistic narratives, *Soul Food, Eve's Bayou, Hav Plenty* (1998), and other contemporary African American films continue the struggle to bring to the screen the vision of independence, self-reliance, and self-actualization that has marked the entire renaissance of African American cinema in the twentieth century.

Conclusion: Gesturing Toward the Millennium

E tiquette and conduct texts are thinly veiled political tracts that attempt to help the reader negotiate social mobility through othering, suppression of "natural" behavior, and, above all, adopting the hegemonic codes espoused by their authors. The body itself is at the center of a struggle for ownership, from the conduct novels of Christine de Pizan to the hybrid conduct novel of Hannah Webster Foster, *The Boarding School*.

The role of social arbiter is itself at the center of a site of struggle for the claim of power. Women and men, African Americans and Europeans have wrestled for the dominion of "social arbiter" for generations. During Reconstruction, we find the voice of Frances E. W. Harper writing *Minnie's Sacrifice*, an African American novel of conduct that usurps the privilege of white power and supremacy. In the Revolutionary period, we find Hannah Webster Foster espousing women's rights to an equal education and championing same-sex friendships in *The Boarding School*. During the nineteenth century, we can locate an outbreak of both male and female writers who used their pens to claim a voice as social arbiters. This suggests the beginning of a gender war for social authority, which is exemplified by the appropriation of the romantic poets who were renarrated, sometimes completely rewritten, as Victorian conduct authors.

At the same time, if we imagine Emily Brontë as a voice of instruction, we can locate a voice of subversion, one that contests gender constructs, heterotopias, and the hegemony of orthodox religion in her poetry in ways that are not unlike those used by Renaissance figures such as Isabella Whitney and Catherine Des Roches. At the same time that white Europeans were involved in a gender war, African American writers and filmmakers were beginning to appropriate the form of the conduct text. Frances E. W. Harper is just one example of this movement. Later, filmmakers such as Oscar Micheaux and Eloyce Gist would use film as a platform to uplift and change American race politics. While Gist and Micheaux were championing (and preaching) to African Americans, white Europeans such as Edith Wharton and Virginia Woolf were critiquing the results of years of stifling white supremacist models of patriarchal behavior. Women filmmakers such as Gist, Lois Weber, Dorothy Reid, and Zora Neale Hurston used the cinema to further question dominant white heterosexist behavior. The twentieth century has seen the legacy of the powerful voices of Emily Post, Amy Vanderbilt, and, more recently, Miss Manners and Martha Stewart, who largely continue to attempt to hold up the standards set by white European models of racial exclusion, gender correction, the foregrounding of heterotopias and heterosexuality, and the promise of social mobility through "correct" behavior. With each wave of social arbiters that attempt to move the public backward toward a false Edenic paradise, we find a number of artists, writers, and filmmakers who form a backlash against the backlash. The rise of Martha Stewart, for example, has been met with derision in performance artist Karen Finley's hysterical book *Living It Up: Humorous Adventures in Hyperdomesticity.* Numerous Web sites have sprung up that attack and critique Martha Stewart as a racist, classist, and sexist throwback. *Just Desserts,* by Jerry Oppenheimer, concludes that Stewart is homophobic, vicious, and a media construct. Quentin Crisp, who assumes the mantle of one of the last "stately Homos of England" has published a number of hysterical send-ups of conduct novels that are not only witty but also models for transgressive behavior that disrupts the hegemonic forces of the past and present. Though the current cinema is plagued by voices of instruction, such as that of Steven Spielberg, who offers *Amistad*—supposedly the first film to tell the story of slavery in America—which stars non–African Americans and erases the historical contributions of African American women in the abolitionist movement, African American filmmakers such as Julie Dash and Kasi Lemmons are making films that tell black stories from a black perspective. With each wave of plantocratic rhetoric comes a wave that corrects and instructs those media-hyped texts of misinformation. Spike Lee's *Four Little Girls* is not only a response to the dominant cinema's exclusion and misinformation on the history of the Civil Rights struggle, but it is a conduct text for and by African American people. It teaches the story of four African American girls who were killed in the Civil Rights struggle and advocates political change and education within the African American community. Kasi Lemmons's *Eve's Bayou* is a conduct text that instructs through narratorial devices that teach African Americans about the complexity of spirituality and sexuality.

The arena of performance art, which is so fraught with political tension, is a remarkably powerful stage for the conduct writer and the performance of social arbitration. The defunding of some NEA artists, including Karen Finley, is a testament to the power of performance art as a vehicle for change. The attacks on the National Endowment for the Arts and the resulting atmosphere of fear within the arts community is a recognition of the power of art as a conduct text. Karen Finley's performance piece, *We Keep Our Victims Ready*, was defunded by the NEA *not* because it is obscene, but because it attacked sexism, homophobia, classism, and the lack of understanding for PWAs (people with AIDS) in the early 1980s. In the summer of 1998, the Whitney Museum canceled a forthcoming show by Finley, scheduled for presentation at the museum. At a performance of her "Return of the Chocolate-Smeared Woman" at the Flea Theatre in New York City in June 1998, Finley spoke out against the Supreme Court ruling that allows the NEA to refuse funding on the basis of "obscene" content. Performance artists such as Karen Finley are engaged in a battle for ownership of the body that can easily be traced to the wars waged by Christine de Pizan over ownership of the female body. Mexican performance artist Guillermo Gómez-Peña is another example of performance artist as conduct writer. His performance piece *El Mexterminator* (created with Roberto Sifuentes) teaches white people how to discuss their fears and desires of Mexicans as a cultural other. *El Mexterminator* includes "Two Live Mexicans" on display at El Museo del Barrio and in performances throughout New York City to provoke public responses. The performers exhibit stereotypes such as hypersexuality, violent behavior, witchcraft, and drug dealing. Appropriating the ethnographic spectacle in which "nonwhite" people are put on spectacle through a white colonialist gaze, Gómez-Peña and Sifuentes turn the gaze around toward the white subject who is encouraged to confess and/or contest his/her honest reactions to Mexican people and Mexican stereotypes. As part of the site-specific exhibit, which includes Mexican velvet paintings, racist American Kitsch, and interactive installations, visitors are encouraged to step up onto a stage, sit on a throne of a bathroom stool, and "perform their favorite cultural other." Rather than preaching values and prohibiting or extolling prescriptive behavioral guides, Gómez-Peña and Sifuentes encourage the viewer/participant to reflect on the injustice of a country perceived to be under siege by immigrants and people of color. The performance/exhibit has the effect of feeling both dangerous and humorous as the viewer/participant comes to perform the role of social arbiter. *El Mexterminator* demonstrates the way in which new technologies such as the Internet may be used to instruct and teach by using the performative arena as a device of self-examination and self-instruction. It is just one example of a new narrative of instructional performative art, and, hopefully, it signals the groundswell of a host of antihegemonic performance heteroglossia to be created in the next millennium.

Works Cited
and Consulted

Index

Works Cited and Consulted

Aresty, Esther B. *The Best Behavior: The Course of Good Manners—From Antiquity to the Present—As Seen Through Courtesy and Etiquette Books*. New York: Simon and Schuster, 1970.

Armstrong, Nancy. "Emily Brontë in and out of Her Time." *Genre* 15.3 (Fall 1982): 243–65.

———. "The Rise of Feminine Authority in the Novel." *Novel* 15.2 (Winter 1982): 127–45.

Armstrong, Nancy, and Leonard Tennenhouse, eds. *The Ideology of Conduct: Essays on Literature and the History of Sexuality*. New York: Methuen, 1987.

———. "The Literature of Conduct, the Conduct of Literature, and the Politics of Desire: An Introduction." *Armstrong and Tennenhouse, Ideology* 2–24.

Ashcroft, Bill, Gareth Griffiths, and Helen Tiffin, eds. *The Postcolonial Studies Reader*. London: Routledge, 1995.

Auerbach, Nina. *Romantic Imprisonment: Women and Other Glorified Outcasts*. New York: Columbia UP, 1985.

Bakhtin, Mikhail (as V. N. Volosinov). *The Dialogic Imagination*. Trans. Caryl Emerson and Michael Holquist. Austin: U of Texas P, 1981.

———. *Marxism and the Philosophy of Language*. Trans. Ladislav Matejka and I. R. Titunik. New York: Seminar, 1973.

———. *Rabelais and His World*. Trans. Hélène Iswolsky. Bloomington: Indiana UP, 1984.

Banerjee, Jacquelin P. "Ambivalence and Contradictions: The Child in Victorian Fiction." *English Studies* 65.6 (December 1984): 481–94.

Barnes, Elizabeth L. "Mirroring the Mother Text: Histories of Seduction in the American Domestic Novel." Singley and Sweeney 157–72.

Beecher, Henry Ward. *Addresses to Young Men*. Philadelphia: Henry Altemus, 1895.

Beilin, Elaine V. *Redeeming Eve: Women Writers of the English Renaissance*. Princeton: Princeton UP, 1987.

Bennett, John, Rev. *Strictures on Female Education*. Rpt. New York: Source Book P, 1971.

Birdwhistell, Ray. *Kinesics and Context: Essays on Body Motion Communication*. Philadelphia: U of Pennsylvania P, 1970.

Bizzell, Patricia, and Bruce Herzberg, eds. *The Rhetorical Tradition: Readings from Classical Times to the Present*. Boston: Bedford, 1990.

Black, Kathleen. *Manners for Moderns*. Boston: Allyn and Bacon, 1938.

Blair, Hugh. *Lectures on Rhetoric and Belles Lettres*. Ed. Harold F. Harding. Carbondale: Southern Illinois UP, 1965.

Blake, William. *The Poetry and Prose of William Blake*. Ed. David V. Erdman. Berkeley: U of California P, 1981.

Blanchard, Joël. "Compilation and Legitimization in the Fifteenth Century: Le Livre de la Cité des Dames." *Reinterpreting Christine de Pizan*. Ed. Earl Jeffrey Richards. Athens: U of Georgia P, 1992. 228–49.

Blau, Herbert. *The Eye of Prey: Subversions of the Postmodern*. Bloomington: Indiana UP, 1987.

Blee, Kathleen M. *Women and the Klan*. Berkeley: U of California P, 1991.

Bloch, Ruth H. "The Gendered Meanings of Virtue in Revolutionary America." *Signs* 13.1 (Fall 1987): 37–57.

Bordo, Susan. "Reading the Male Body." Goldstein 265–306.

Bornstein, Diane, ed. "Humanism in Christine de Pisan's *Livre du Corps de Policie*." *Les Bonnes Feuilles* 3 (1974): 100–115.

———. *The Lady in the Tower: Medieval Courtesy Literature for Women*. Hamden, CT: Archon Books, 1983.

———. *Mirrors of Courtesy*. Hamden, CT: Archon Books, 1975.

Bornstein, Kate. *Gender Outlaw: On Men, Women and the Rest of Us*. New York: Vintage, 1994.

Bowser, Eileen. *The History of American Cinema II: The Transformation of Cinema 1907–1915*. New York: Scribner's, 1990.

Bronfen, Elisabeth. *Over Her Dead Body: Configurations of Femininity, Death and the Aesthetic*. New York: Routledge, 1992.

Brontë, Emily Jane. *The Complete Poems of Emily Jane Brontë*. Ed. C. W. Hatfield. New York: Columbia UP, 1941.

The Brontës: Their Lives, Friendships and Correspondence. Ed. T. J. Wise and J. A. Symington. 4 vols. Oxford: Shakespeare Head, 1932.

Brownlee, Kevin. "Discourses of the Self: Christine de Pizan and *The Rose*." *Romanic Review* 79.1 (1977): 199–221.

Butler, Judith. "Performative Acts and Gender Constitution: An Essay in Phenomenology and Feminist Theory." Case 270–82.

Bynum, Caroline Walker. *Holy Feast and Holy Fast: The Religious Significance of Food to Medieval Women*. Berkeley: U of California P, 1986.

———. *Jesus as Mother: Studies in the Spirituality of the High Middle Ages*. Berkeley: U of California P, 1982.

Carson, Gerald. *The Polite Americans: 300 Years of More or Less Good Behaviour*. London: Macmillan, 1967.

Case, Sue-Ellen, ed. *Performing Feminisms: Feminist Critical Theory and Theatre*. Baltimore: John Hopkins UP, 1990.

Case, Sue-Ellen, Philip Brett, and Susan Leigh Foster, eds. *Cruising the Performative: Interventions into the Representation of Ethnicity, Nationality and Sexuality*. Bloomington: Indiana UP, 1995.

Castiglione, Baldassare. *The Book of the Courtier*. Trans. George Bull. New York: Penguin, 1967.

Chance, Jane. *Christine de Pizan's Letter of Othea to Hector: Translated with Introduction, Notes, and Interpretative Essay*. Newburyport, MA: Focus, 1990.

Charnov, Elaine S. "Zora Neale Hurston: A Pioneer in Visual Anthropology." Paper presented at the Second Annual Zora Neale Hurston Festival of the Arts and Humanities, 1991.

Cixous, Hélène. "The Laugh of the Medusa." *Signs* 1.4 (Summer 1976): 875–94.

Clark, Katerina, and Michael Holquist. *Mikhail Bakhtin.* Cambridge: Harvard UP, 1984.

Connell, R. W. *Gender and Power: Society, the Person and Sexual Politics.* Cambridge: Polity, 1987.

Correll, Barbara. "The Politics of Civility in Renaissance Texts: Grobiana in Grobianus." *Exemplaria* 2.2 (Fall 1990): 627–58.

Crowninshield, Francis W. *Manners for the Metropolis.* New York: Arno, 1975.

Curtin, Michael. "A Question of Manners: Status and Gender in Etiquette and Courtesy." *Journal of Modern History* 67.3 (September 1985): 395–423.

Delany, Sheila. *Medieval Literary Politics: Shapes of Ideology.* Manchester: St. Martin's, 1990.

De Marinis, Marco. *The Semiotics of Performance.* Trans. Áine O'Healy. Bloomington: Indiana UP, 1993.

de Pizan, Christine. *The Book of Fayttes of Armes and of Chyualrye Translated and Printed by William Caxton from the French Original by Christine de Pisan.* Ed. A. T. P. Byles. London: Oxford UP, 1937.

———. *The Book of the City of Ladies.* Trans. Earl Jeffrey Richards. New York: Persea, 1982.

———. *The 'Epistle of Othea' Translated from the French Text of Christine de Pisan by Stephen Scrope.* Ed. C. F. Bühler. Oxford: Oxford UP, 1970.

———. *The Middle English Translation of Christine de Pisan's 'Livre du Corps de Policie: ed. from M S C.U.L.K.k. 1.5* Ed. Diane Bornstein. Heidelberg: Carl Winter, 1977.

———. *The Treasure of the City of Ladies or the Book of Three Virtues.* Trans. Sarah Lawson. London: Penguin, 1985.

Dimock, Wai-Chee. "Debasing Exchange: Edith Wharton's *The House of Mirth.*" *PMLA* 100.5 (October 1985): 783–91.

Dobson, Joanne. "The Hidden Hand: Subversion of Cultural Ideology in Three Mid-Nineteenth-Century American Women's Novels." *American Quarterly* 38.2 (Summer 1986): 223–42.

Donovan, Josephine. "Women and the Rise of the Novel." *Signs* 16 (Spring 1991): 441–62.

Doyle, Jennifer, Jonathan Flatley, and Jose Esbeban Muñoz, eds. *Pop Out: Queer Warhol.* Durham: Duke UP, 1996.

Duffy, Richard. "Introduction: Manners and Morals." *Emily Post's Etiquette: In Society, in Business, in Politics and at Home.* By Emily Price Post. New York: Funk and Wagnalls, 1922. i–xvii.

Elias, Norbert. *The History of Manners.* Trans. Edmund Jephcott. New York: Pantheon, 1978.

Ellul, Jacques. *Propaganda: The Formation of Men's Attitudes.* Trans. Konrad Kellen and Jean Lerner. New York: Knopf, 1965.

Erkila, Betsy. *The Wicked Sisters: Women Poets, Literary History and Discord.* New York: Oxford, 1992.

Erkila, Betsy, and Jay Grossman, eds. *Breaking Bounds: Whitman and American Cultural Studies.* New York: Oxford UP, 1996.

Erler, Mary, and Maryanne Kowalski, eds. *Women and Power in the Middle Ages.* Athens: U of Georgia P, 1998.

Faderman, Lillian. *Surpassing the Love of Men: Romantic Friendship and Love Between Women, from the Renaissance to the Present.* New York: Morrow, 1981.

Farwell, Marilyn R. "Toward a Definition of the Lesbian Literary Imagination." *Signs* 14.11 (Fall 1988): 100–18.

Feher, Michel, Ramona Naddaff, and Nadia Tazi, eds. *Fragments for a History of the Human Body.* New York: Zone, 1989.

Feinberg, Leslie. *Transgender Warriors: Making History from Joan of Arc to RuPaul.* Boston: Beacon, 1996.

Fenwick, Millicent. *Vogue's Book of Etiquette: A Complete Guide to Traditional Forms of Modern Usage.* New York: Simon, 1948.

Finke, Laurie. "Mystical Bodies and the Dialogics of Vision." *Philological Quarterly* 67.4 (Fall 1988): 439–50.

Finkelstein, Joanne. *Dining Out: A Sociology of Modern Manners.* Oxford: Polity, 1989.

Finley, Karen. *Living It Up: Humorous Adventures in Hyperdomesticity.* New York: Doubleday, 1996.

Fletcher, John, and Andrew Benjamin, eds. *Abjection, Melancholia and Love: The Work of Julia Kristeva.* New York: Routledge, 1990.

Flynn, Carol Houlihan. "Defoe's Idea of Conduct: Ideological Fictions and Fictional Reality." Armstrong and Tennenhouse, *Ideology* 73–96.

Forte, Jeanie. "Women's Performance Art: Feminism and Postmodernism." *Performing Feminisms: Feminist Critical Theory and Theatre.* Case 251–69.

Foster, Frances Smith. Introduction. *Minnie's Sacrifice: Sowing and Reaping, Trial and Triumph.* By Frances E. W. Harper. Ed. Frances Smith Foster. Boston: Beacon, 1994. xi–xxxvii.

Foster, Gwendolyn Audrey. "Troping the Body: Etiquette Texts and Performance." *Text and Performance Quarterly* 13.1 (January 1993): 79–96.

———. *Women Film Directors: An International Bio-Critical Dictionary.* Westport, CT: Greenwood, 1995.

Foster, Hannah Webster. *The Boarding School: or, Lessons of a Preceptress to Her Pupils: Consisting of Information, Instruction, and Advice. Calculated to Improve the Manners, and Form the Character of Young Ladies, to Which Is Added a Collection of LETTERS, Written by the Pupils, to Their INSTRUCTOR, Their FRIENDS and Each Other.* Boston: I. Thomas and E. T. Andrews, 1798.

Foster, Jeannette. *Sex Variant Women in Literature.* Baltimore: Diana Press, 1975.

Foucault, Michel. *The Care of the Self.* Trans. Robert Hurley. New York: Pantheon, 1986.

———. *Discipline and Punish: The Birth of the Prison.* Trans. Alan Sheridan. New York: Pantheon, 1977.

———. *The History of Sexuality.* Trans. Robert Hurley. Harmondsworth: Penguin, 1981.

———. *The Order of Things.* New York: Pantheon, 1971.

———. *The Use of Pleasure.* Trans. Robert Hurley. New York: Pantheon, 1985.

Frank, Katherine. *A Chainless Soul: A Life of Emily Brontë*. Boston: Houghton, 1990.

Friedberg, Anne. *Window Shopping: Cinema and the Postmodern*. Berkeley: U of California P, 1993.

Gallant, Christine. "The Archetypal Feminine in Emily Brontë's Poetry." *WS* 7.1, 2 (1980): 85–89.

Gates, Henry Louis, Jr., ed. *"Race," Writing and Difference*. Chicago: U of Chicago P, 1986.

Giddens, Anthony. *Modernity and Self Identity: Self and Society in the Late Modern Age*. Stanford: Stanford UP, 1991.

Goldstein, Laurence, ed. *The Male Body: Features, Destinies, Exposures*. Ann Arbor: U of Michigan P, 1994.

Gómez-Peña, Guillermo, and Roberto Sifuentes. *Temple of Confessions*. Detroit: Powerhouse/Detroit Institute of Arts, 1996.

Graf, Fritz. "Gestures and Conventions: The Gestures of Roman Actors and Orators." *A Cultural History of Gesture*. Ed. Jan Bremmer and Herman Roodenberg. Ithaca: Cornell UP, 1991. 36–58.

Gregory, John. *A Father's Legacy to His Daughters*. Rpt. New York: Garland, 1974.

Griffin, Walter T., ed. *The Homes of Our Country, or the Centers of Moral and Religious Influence; The Crystals of Society; The Nuclei of National Character*. New York: Chas. L. Snyder, 1882.

Hall, Kim F. "Sexual Politics and Cultural Identity in *The Masque of Blackness*." *The Performance of Power: Theatrical Discourse and Politics*. Ed. Sue-Ellen Case and Janelle Reinelt. Iowa City: U of Iowa P, 1991. 3–18.

Hamilton, Kristie. "An Assault on the Will: Republican Virtue and the City in Hannah Webster Foster's *The Coquette*." *Early American Literature* 24.2 (1989): 135–51.

Harper, Frances E. W. *Minnie's Sacrifice, Sowing and Reaping, Trial and Triumph*. Ed. Frances Smith Foster. Boston: Beacon, 1994.

Harris, Sharon M., ed. *Redefining the Political Novel: American Women Writers 1797–1901*. Knoxville: U of Tennessee P, 1995.

Harris, Wendell. "Romantic Bard and Victorian Commentators: The Meaning and Significance of Meaning and Significance." *Victorian Poetry* 24.4 (Winter 1986): 455–69.

Harrison, Daphne Duval. *Black Pearls: Blues Queens of the 1920s*. New Brunswick: Rutgers UP, 1988.

Herdt, Gilbert. *Third Sex, Third Gender: Beyond Sexual Dimorphism in Culture and History*. New York: Zone, 1994.

Herndl, Diane Price. "The Dilemmas of a Feminine Dialogic." *Feminism, Bakhtin, and the Dialogic*. Ed. Dale Bauer and S. McKinstry. Albany: SUNY P, 1991. 7–24.

Hill, Thomas E. *Hill's Manual of Social and Business Forms: A Guide to Correct Writing, with Approved Methods in Speaking and Acting in the Various Relations of Life, Embracing Instruction and Examples in Penmanship, Spelling, Use of Capital Letters, Punctuation, Composition, Writing for the Press, Proof-Reading, Epistolary Correspondence, Notes of Invitations, Cards, Commercial Forms, Legal Business Forms, Family Records, Synonyms, Short-Hand Writing, Duties of Secretaries, Parliamentary Rules, Sign-Writing, Epitaphs, the Laws of Etiquette, Book Keeping, Valuable Tables of Reference, Writing Poetry, Etc. Etc.* Chicago: Hill, 1891.

Hodge, Robert, and Gunther Kress. *Social Semiotics.* Oxford: Polity, 1988.

Holt, Emily. *Encyclopedia of Etiquette.* Garden City: Doubleday, 1921.

Homans, Margaret. *Women Writers and Poetic Identity: Dorothy Wordsworth, Emily Brontë, and Emily Dickinson.* Princeton: Princeton UP, 1980.

hooks, bell. *Reel to Real: Race, Sex, and Class at the Movies.* New York: Routledge, 1996.

Hunt, Lynn. *The Invention of Pornography: Obscenity and the Origins of Modernity, 1500–1800.* New York: Zone, 1993.

James, Janet Wilson. *Changing Ideas about Women in the United States.* New York: Garland, 1981.

Jarman, Franklin M. "The Young Executive Between Two Worlds." *Corporate Etiquette.* By Milla Alihan. New York: NAL, 1970. i–vii.

Jarratt, Susan. "Performing Feminism, Histories, Rhetorics." *Rhetoric Society Quarterly* 22.1 (Winter 1992): 111–32.

Jones, Ann Rosalind. "Nets and Bridles: Early Modern Conduct Books and Sixteenth-Century Women's Lyrics." Armstrong and Tennenhouse, *Ideology* 39–72.

Kaplan, E. Ann. "Madonna Politics: Perversion, Repression, or Subversion? Or Masks and/as Master-y." *The Madonna Connection: Representational Politics, Subcultural Identities, and Cultural Theory.* Ed. Cathy Schwichtenberg. San Francisco: Westview, 1993. 149–66.

Kasson, John F. *Rudeness and Civility: Manners in Nineteenth-Century America.* New York: Farrar, 1990.

Kemp, Sandra. "'But how describe a world seen without a self?' Feminism, Fiction and Modernism." *Critical Quarterly* 32.1 (Spring 1990): 99–118.

Kennedy, Stetson. *Jim Crow Guide to the U.S.A.: The Laws, Customs and Etiquette Governing the Conduct of Nonwhites and Other Minorities as Second-Class Citizens.* London: Lawrence and Wishart, 1959.

Kerber, Linda. *Women of the Republic: Intellect and Ideology in Revolutionary America.* New York: Norton, 1986.

King, William O., ed. *Portraits and Principles of the World's Great Men and Women with Practical Lessons on Successful Life by Over Fifty Leading Thinkers.* Springfield: King-Richardson, 1896.

Kochman, Thomas. "The Politics of Politeness: Social Warrants in Mainstream American Public Etiquette." *Georgetown University Round Table on Languages and Linguistics 1984; Meaning, Form, and Use in Context: Linguistic Applications.* Ed. Deborah Schiffrin. Washington, D.C.: Georgetown UP, 1984. 200–209.

Kristeva, Julia. "The Adolescent Novel." Fletcher and Benjamin 8–23.

———. *Language: The Unknown: An Initiation into Linguistics.* Trans. Anne M. Menke. New York: Columbia UP, 1989.

———. *Powers of Horror: An Essay on Abjection.* Trans. Peon Roudiez. New York: Columbia UP, 1985.

Kroker, Arthur, and Marilouise Kroker, eds. *The Last Sex: Feminism and Outlaw Bodies.* New York: St. Martins, 1993.

Laennec, Christine Moneera. "Christine Antygrate: Authorial Ambivalence in the Works of Christine de Pizan." Singley and Sweeney 35–49.

Langer, Ullrich. "Merit in Courtly Literature: Castiglione, Rabelais, Marguerite de Navarre, and Le Caron." *Renaissance Quarterly* 16.2 (Summer 1988): 218–41.

Leighton, Angela. *Victorian Women Poets: Writing Against the Heart.* Charlottesville: UP of Virginia, 1992.

Lockridge, Laurence S. *The Ethics of Romanticism.* Cambridge: Cambridge UP, 1989.

Long, Beverly Whitaker. "Performance Criticism and Questions of Value," *Text and Performance Quarterly* 2.2 (April 1991): 106–15.

Lynes, Russell. "How America Invented Manners." *Saturday Evening Post* 22–29 December 1962: 10, 12.

Mack, P. "Women as Prophets During the English Civil War." *Feminist Studies* 8 (Spring 1982): 19–5.

Mahbobhah, Albaraq. "Reading the Anorexic Maze." *Genders* 14 (Fall 1992): 87–97.

Marin, Louis. "The Gesture of Looking in Classical Historical Painting." *History and Anthropology* 1.1 (November 1984): 175–91.

Marion, J. H., Jr. "Courtesy Across the Color Line." *Christian Century* 15 May 1940: 638–39.

Markun, Leo. *Mrs. Grundy: A History of Four Centuries of Morals Intended to Illuminate Present Problems in Great Britain and the United States.* New York: Appleton, 1930.

Marshall, William. *Nature as a Book of Symbols.* New York: Hunt and Eaton, 1895.

Martin, Judith. "Why Manners Matter." *Harper's* Aug. 1984: 35.

Mather, Cotton. *Bethiah: The Glory Which Adorns the Daughters of God and the Piety, Wherewith ZION Wishes to See Her Daughters Glorious.* Boston: Franklin for Gerrish, 1722.

———. *Ornaments for the Daughters of Zion. Or the Character and Happiness of a Virtuous Woman.* Rpt. New York: Delmar, 1978.

Maynard, John. *Charlotte Brontë and Sexuality.* Cambridge: Cambridge UP, 1984.

McCrady, Marjorie Ellis, and Blanche Wheeler. *Manners for Moderns.* New York: Dutton, 1942.

Mellor, Anne K. *Romanticism and Gender.* New York: Routledge, 1993.

Melville, Stephen, and Bill Readings, eds. *Vision and Textuality.* Durham: Duke UP, 1995.

Mill, John Stuart. *On Liberty.* Garden City: Doubleday, 1961.

Miller, Alice Duer. "I Like American Manners." *Saturday Evening Post* 13 August 1932: 5, 43.

Minow-Pinkney, Makiko, "Virginia Woolf: 'Seen from a Foreign Land.'" Fletcher and Benjamin 157–77.

Mitchell, Sally. *The New Girl: Girls' Culture in England, 1880–1915.* New York: Columbia UP, 1995.

Moi, Toril. *Sexual/Textual Politics: Feminist Literary Theory.* New York: Routledge, 1985.

Newman, Beth. "'The Situation of the Looker-On': Gender, Narration, and Gaze in *Wuthering Heights.*" *PMLA* 105.5 (October 1990): 1029–41.

Newton, Judith Lowder. *Women, Power and Subversion: Social Strategies in*

British Fiction, 1778–1860. Athens: U of Georgia P, 1987.

Newton, Sarah Emily. "Wise and Foolish Virgins: 'Usable Fiction' and the Early American Conduct Tradition." *Early American Literature* 25 (1990): 137–67.

Ogden, Annegret S. *The Great American Housewife from Helpmate to Wage Earner, 1776–1986.* Westport: Greenwood P, 1986.

Oppenheimer, Jerry. *Just Desserts: The Unauthorized Biography of Martha Stewart.* New York: Morrow, 1997.

Panofsky, Richard. "Love Poetry of Isabella Whitney: A Woman Author of the English Renaissance." *New Mexico Highlands University Journal* 6.1 (April 1983): 1–8.

Payne, C. H. *Guides and Guards in Character Building.* New York: Phillips and Hunt, 1883.

Pettengill, Claire C. "Sisterhood in a Separate Sphere: Female Friendship in Hannah Webster Foster's *The Coquette* and *The Boarding School*." *Early American Literature* 27 (1992): 185–203.

Pogrebin, Robin. "Master of Her Own Destiny, for Martha Stewart, a One-Woman Show with Many Flourishes." *New York Times* 8 February 1998: 3.1, 14.

Porritt, Ruth. "Surpassing Derrida's Deconstructed Self: Virginia Woolf's Poetic Disarticulation of the Self." *Women's Studies* 21.3 (Summer 1992): 323–39.

Post, Elizabeth L. *The Emily Post Book of Etiquette for Young People.* New York: Funk and Wagnalls, 1967.

Post, Emily Price. *Emily Post's Etiquette: In Society, in Business, in Politics and at Home.* New York: Funk and Wagnalls, 1922.

———. *Etiquette: The Blue Book of Social Usage.* New York: Funk and Wagnalls, 1927.

Quilligan, Maureen. "Allegory and the Textual Body: Female Authority in Christine de Pizan's *Livre de la Cite des Dames*." *Romanic Review* 79.1 (1988): 222–48.

———. *The Allegory of Female Authority: Christine de Pizan's Cité Des Dames.* Ithaca: Cornell UP, 1991.

Quintilian, Marcus Fabius. *Institutes of Oratory.* Trans. H. E. Butler. 4 vols. New York: Loeb Classical Library, 1921.

Raymond, George Lansing. *Poetry as a Representative Art: An Essay in Comparative Aesthetics.* New York: Putnam, 1886.

Rayne, M. L., ed. *Written for You, or, The Art of Beautiful Living.* Detroit: Tyler, 1882.

"A Remarkable Monument to Wally Reid's Memory," *Photoplay* (September 1924): 105–7.

Richardson, Alan. "Romanticism and the Colonization of the Feminine." Ed. Anne K. Mellor. *Romanticism and Feminism.* Bloomington: Indiana UP, 1988. 13–25.

Rony, Fatimah Tobing. *The Third Eye: Race, Cinema and Ethnographic Spectacle.* Durham, NC: Duke UP, 1996.

Roof, Judith. *Come as You Are: Sexuality and Narrative.* New York: Columbia UP, 1996.

Ross, Kristin. *Fast Cars, Clean Bodies: Decolonization and the Reordering of French Culture.* Cambridge: MIT, 1995.

Ruskin, John. *Pearls for Young Ladies*. New York: Caldwell, 1878.

Schmitt, Jean-Claude. "The Ethics of Gesture." Feher, Naddaff, and Tazi 129–47.

Schor, Naomi. "Female Fetishism: The Case of George Sand." *The Female Body in Western Culture*. Ed. Susan Rubin Suleiman. Cambridge: Harvard UP, 1986. 363–72.

Sedgwick, Eve Kosofsky. *Epistemology of the Closet*. Berkeley: U of California P, 1990.

———. *Tendencies*. Durham: Duke UP, 1993.

Seidler, Victor J. *Rediscovering Masculinity: Reason, Language and Sexuality*. London: Routledge, 1989.

Singley, Carol J., and Susan Elizabeth Sweeney, eds. *Anxious Power*. Albany: SUNY P, 1993.

Slide, Anthony. *Early Women Directors*. New York: Da Capo, 1984.

———. *Lois Weber: The Director Who Lost Her Way in Hollywood*. Westport, CT: Greenwood, 1996.

Sloan, Kay. "The Hand That Rocks the Cradle: An Introduction." *Film History* 1.4 (1987): 341–42.

Smith-Rosenberg, Carroll. "Domesticating 'Virtue': Coquettes and Revolutionaries in Young America." *Literature and The Body: Essays on Populations and Persons*. Ed. Elaine Scarry. Baltimore: John Hopkins UP, 1986: 160–84.

Sprackling, Helen. *Courtesy: A Book of Modern Manners*. New York: Barrows, 1947.

Staiger, Janet. "The Politics of Film Canons." *Multiple Voices in Feminist Film Criticism*. Ed. Diane Carson, Linda Dittmar, and Janice Welsch. Minneapolis: U of Minnesota P, 1994. 191–209.

Stallybrass, Peter. "Patriarchal Territories: The Body Enclosed." *Rewriting the Renaissance*. Ed. Margaret W. Ferguson, Maureen Quilligan, and Nancy Vickers. Chicago: U of Chicago P, 1986. 123–42.

Strasser, Susan. *Never Done: A History of American Housework*. New York: Pantheon, 1982.

Stratton, Dorothy C., and Helen B. Schleman. *Your Best Foot Forward: Social Usage for Young Moderns*. New York: Whittlesey, 1940.

Taylor, Nancy. *Nancy Taylor: Book IV*. N.p., n.d.

Tennyson, Alfred. *Tennyson's Poetry*. Ed. Robert W. Hill Jr. New York: Norton, 1971.

Titcomb, Timothy, [Josiah Gilbert Holland]. *Titcomb's Letters to Young People Single and Married*. New York: Scribner's, 1871.

Travitsky, Betty. "The Lady Doth Protest: Protest in Popular Writings of Renaissance Englishwomen." *English Literary Renaissance* 14 (Fall 1984): 255–83.

———, ed. *The Paradise of Women: Writings by Englishwomen of the Renaissance*. Westport, CT: Greenwood P, 1981.

———. "The Wyll and Testament of Isabella Whitney." *English Literary Renaissance* 10 (Winter 1980): 76–94.

Trinh T. Minh-ha. *Woman, Native, Other: Writing Postcoloniality and Feminism*. Bloomington: Indiana UP, 1989.

Twigg, Reginald. "Aestheticizing the Home: Textual Strategies of Taste, Self Identity, and Bourgeois Hegemony in America's 'Gilded Age.'" *Text and Performance Quarterly* (January 1992): 1–20.

Vanderbilt, Amy. *Amy Vanderbilt's Complete Book of Etiquette: A Guide to Gracious Living*. Garden City: Doubleday, 1952.

Vigarello, Georges. "The Upward Training of the Body from the Age of Chivalry to Courtly Civility." Feher, Naddaff, and Tazi 149–209.

Visser, Margaret. *The Rituals of Dinner*. New York: Penguin, 1991.

Vogue's Book of Etiquette: Present-Day Customs of Social Intercourse with the Rules for Their Correct Observance. Garden City: Doubleday, 1935.

Waid, Candace. *Edith Wharton's Letters from the Underworld: Fictions of Women and Writing*. Chapel Hill: U of North Carolina P, 1991.

Wall, Wendy. "Isabella Whitney and the Female Legacy." *ELH* 58.1 (Spring 1991): 35–62.

———. "Our Bodies/Our Texts? Renaissance Women and the Trials of Authorship." Singley and Sweeney 51–71.

Wang, Ban. "'I' on the Run: Crisis of Identity in Mrs. Dalloway." *Modern Fiction Studies* 38.1 (Spring 1992): 177–92.

Waugh, Thomas. "Cultivated Colonies: Notes on Queer Nationhood and the Erotic Image." *Canadian Journal of Film Studies* 2.2/3 (1993): 145–78.

West, Jane. *Letters to a Young Lady in Which the Duties and Character of Women Are Considered*. 3 Vols. Rpt. New York: Garland, 1974.

Wharton, Edith. *A Backward Glance*. New York: Scribner's, 1964.

———. *The House of Mirth*. New York: Bantam, 1984.

Wheatley, Phillis. *The Collected Works of Phillis Wheatley*. Ed. John Shields. New York: Oxford UP, 1988.

Willard, Charity Cannon. *Christine de Pizan: Her Life and Works*. New York: Persea, 1984.

Wilson, Katharina M., ed. *Medieval Woman Writers*. Athens: U of Georgia P, 1984.

Wolff, Cynthia Griffin. *A Feast of Words: The Triumph of Edith Wharton*. New York: Oxford U P, 1977.

Wollstonecraft, Mary. *A Vindication of the Rights of Woman* (1792); and John Stuart Mill. *The Subjection of Women* (1869). London: Dent, 1970.

Woodring, Carl. *Politics in English Romantic Poetry*. Cambridge: Harvard UP, 1970.

Woods, E. M. *The Negro in Etiquette: A Novelty*. St. Louis: Buxton and Skinner, 1899.

Woolf, Virginia. *Moments of Being*. Ed. Jeanne Schulkind. San Diego: Harcourt, 1985.

———. *Mrs. Dalloway*. San Diego: Harcourt, 1981.

———. *A Writer's Diary*. New York: Harcourt, 1953.

Wordsworth, William. *The Poetical Works of William Wordsworth*. Ed. Edward De Selincourt. 5 vols. Oxford: Oxford UP, 1940–49.

———. *William Wordsworth: The Prelude 1799, 1805, 1850*. Ed. Jonathan Wordsworth, M. H. Abrams, and Stephen Gill. New York: Norton, 1979.

Woudhuysen, H. R., ed. *The Penguin Book of Renaissance Verse*. London: Penguin, 1993.

Young, Iris Marion, ed. *Throwing Like a Girl and Other Essays in Feminist Philosophy and Social Theory*. Bloomington: Indiana UP, 1990.

Zavarzadeh, Mas'ud. *Seeing Films Politically*. Albany: SUNY P, 1991.

Index

Gwendolyn Audrey Foster is an associate professor of film studies and cultural studies in the Department of English at the University of Nebraska, Lincoln. Her books include *Women Film Directors: An International Bio-Critical Dictionary*; *Women Filmmakers of the African and Asian Diaspora: De/Colonizing the Gaze, Locating Subjectivity*; and *Captive Bodies: Postcolonial Subjectivity in Cinema*. Foster wrote and directed *The Women Who Made the Movies*, a documentary on early women film directors. She received the Emerging Scholar Award from the American Association of University Women in 1999.